MW01196155

PRAISE FOR
ETERNAL HEART

"Carl McColman offers us another gift of contemplative insight and illumination. He encourages us to embrace in our own lives this mystical gift and vision and charts the way through accessible practices. Reading it left my heart kindled by both joy and possibility."

—Christine Valters Paintner, PhD, author of
fifteen books, including *Breath Prayer: An
Ancient Practice for the Everyday Sacred*

"There is no better time than now to delve into the subject of the heart. Carl McColman leads us further into our hearts as sleuths in the mystery of life. What joy!"

—Zenju Earthlyn Manuel, ordained Zen Buddhist priest
and author of several books, including *The Deepest
Peace: Contemplations from a Season of Stillness*

"Moving through the chapters of *Eternal Heart* is like praying with a string of smooth beads. Each one invites a sacred pause, and together they are a work of prayerful beauty."

—The Rev. Dr. Stuart Higginbotham, Episcopal
priest and author of *The Heart of a Calling*

"McColman invites us to reencounter love, silence, courage, renewal, and other gifts of the heart that engender sustaining hope and joy."

—Lisa Colón DeLay, host of the *Spark My Muse*
podcast and author of *The Wild Land Within*

"A sustained rhapsody on every aspect of the spiritual life, woven in a language full of insight, speaking directly to the love-hungry heart."

—Paul Quenon, OCSO, poet, Cistercian monk, and author of *Unquiet Vigil* and *In Praise of the Useless Life*

"A generous invitation to enter into the heart of the mystery. Carl McColman offers a lens of love through which to gaze upon eternal gifts hidden in the very center of all that is. Such sacred seeing transforms what it beholds."

—Mirabai Starr, author of *God of Love* and *Wild Mercy*

"*Eternal Heart* shows us how to seek what is eternal and sacred in all things. It is a book whose 'heart practices' we will feel drawn to repeatedly over the different seasons of our lives."

—Judith Valente, author of *How to Be: What the Rule of St. Benedict Teaches Us about Happiness, Meaning, and Community* and *Atchison Blue: A Search for Silence, a Spiritual Home, and a Living Faith*

"*Eternal Heart* is a work of humanly sung companionship, as timely as it is transcendent. Carl McColman reminds us that becoming more truly human is the first step toward a fruitful and contemporary holiness."

—Therese Schroeder-Sheker, musician and author of *Transitus: A Blessed Death in the Modern World*

"Mysticism and contemplation can feel abstract and challenging, but *Eternal Heart* grounds ancient practices in concepts familiar to everyone. This book helps our hearts find a path toward the things they most long for."

—Kaya Oakes, author of *Radical Reinvention*

"In *Eternal Heart*, Carl McColman illuminates the pathway of the heart with wisdom, ease, and a touch of joy, inviting us into eternal possibility. *Eternal Heart* shines a light on ways of seeing that can bring us closer to divine presence."

—Colette Lafia, author of *The Divine Heart: Seven Ways to Live in God's Love* and *Seeking Surrender*

"Carl McColman invites readers to travel with him on a journey well paved by ancient mystics and contemporary sages. McColman himself is a wise guide, leading us into an awakened heart."

—Christiana N. Peterson, author of *Awakened by Death* and *Mystics and Misfits*

"With beauty and simplicity, Carl McColman opens the gifts of the heart, encouraging us to receive the blessings that sometimes lie hidden until we're able to see them anew."

—Lisa Deam, author of *3000 Miles to Jesus: Pilgrimage as a Way of Life for Spiritual Seekers*

"Carl McColman makes a compelling case for why more of us should claim and embrace the mystical path. And he provides the encouragement and wisdom we need to go deeper on this journey."

—Kate H. Rademacher, author of *Reclaiming Rest: The Promise of Sabbath, Solitude, and Stillness in a Restless World*

"*Eternal Heart* is a beautiful offering that not only informs us about what contemplation is but also gives us a felt sense of its quiet aliveness and joy. Reading it feels like listening to a gentle call. This book is not only meant to be read but also prayed."

—The Rev. Adam Bucko, co-author of *Occupy Spirituality* and *The New Monasticism*

ADDITIONAL PRAISE FOR CARL McCOLMAN

"Carl McColman's first gift is his commitment to write about things that matter. His second gift is his ability to write about them with clarity and warmth. He leads us to the brink of lessons no book can teach, then frees us to go forward to learn them."

—Barbara Brown Taylor, author of *Holy Envy*

"Carl McColman gives you much wise direction. Here is your teacher!"

—Richard Rohr, author of *Universal Christ*

"Carl McColman presents the classic precepts and practices of the Christian contemplative path in a clear and helpful way."

—Cynthia Bourgeault, author of *The Heart of Centering Prayer*

"Carl McColman obviously earned his understanding of mysticism through years of research, as well as his own personal spiritual journey, and there is no more powerful combination for inspired writing."

—Carolyn Myss, author of *Anatomy of the Spirit*

"Carl McColman masterfully maps out for the serious spiritual seeker the nature of the mystical experience and outlines a clear and accessible pathway for how to get there."

—Kyriacos C. Markides, author of *The Mountain of Silence*

ETERNAL HEART

ETERNAL HEART

THE MYSTICAL PATH TO
A JOYFUL LIFE

CARL
McCOLMAN

BROADLEAF BOOKS
MINNEAPOLIS

ETERNAL HEART
The Mystical Path to a Joyful Life

Cover image: Ripitya/shutterstock
Cover design: Gearbox

Print ISBN: 978-1-5064-6461-9
eBook ISBN: 978-1-5064-6462-6

CONTENTS

For three friends who embody the
wisdom of their eternal hearts:
Linda Boland
Linda Mitchell
Sr. LaVerne Peter, WSHS

0

INFINITY

Sometimes the key to opening up possibilities in life can come from something as simple as learning to see things from a new perspective.

For a rather playful example of this, consider the number eight. If you tip it on its side, it opens up into infinity, like this:

$$8 \quad \infty$$

I know this is hardly earth-shattering; indeed, it is something everyone who has ever learned even basic mathematics has figured out. Probably every teacher who has ever taught a class how to make an infinity symbol has had to deal with the smart-alecky kid in the back corner saying, "That's just a figure eight on its side!"

I was that kid. Incidentally, the technical name for the infinity symbol is a lemniscate, referring to any type of figure-eight curve that can be calculated in algebraic geometry. (Incidentally, one of the first philosophers to study the mathematics of the lemniscate was the pagan mystic Proclus, who influenced the early Christian contemplative writer Dionysius the Pseudo-Areopagite.)

Human ideas, thought, and imagination all get codified in symbols—letters, numbers, punctuation, and algebraic symbols—and we use these symbols to create mathematics and language, to communicate, to ponder, to speculate, and to wonder. And here we have two symbols that are essentially the same thing, only the orientation is different. You can find other examples of this, such as the letter *M* and the Greek letter sigma, Σ, which also shows up as a mathematical symbol. But for now, let's just linger with eight and infinity.

Consider these lovely words from the poet William Blake:

> *To see a World in a Grain of Sand*
> *And a Heaven in a Wild Flower:*
> *Hold Infinity in the palm of your hand*
> *And Eternity in an hour.*

Spiritual life thrives when we see things from new angles and perspectives, when we open up to make connections we didn't notice before, when we imagine new possibilities and potentialities. And then we not only see these hidden possibilities, but by the grace of God they can help us make choices and commitments that generate blessings for all.

Tip infinity on its side and it looks like the number eight. Eight is hardly infinite; truly it's an unassuming number. Everyone loves three ("third time is the charm"), seven gets to boast about being the number of chakras or sacraments, and nine gets repeated ad nauseam on the worst song the Beatles ever recorded. But poor eight, its only claim to fame is that it equals two cubed $(2 \times 2 \times 2)$. And yet hidden in this most humble of numbers is the symbol of infinity itself. But you have to look at it sideways to see the possibility that a new perspective brings.

The wisdom of seeing things from a different perspective has ramifications far beyond the trick of moving characters on a page. Vietnamese Buddhist monk Thich Nhat Hanh talks about a concept he calls "interbeing"— a way of learning to see how everything is connected. If you are reading a hard copy of this book, consider how the paper comes from a tree that grew in a forest or a tree farm, a real place with a real physical location. That tree lived and grew for years, nurtured by the sun, the soil, the rain. Looking at this (or any) sheet of paper, you recognize that the sunlight and the dirt and water wove together to make this piece of paper possible.

Take a step back further and consider how pretty much everything that exists is fashioned of the cosmos itself—stardust. When the electronica musician Moby sang, "We are all made of stars," he was telling the truth.

Interbeing exists whether we notice it or not. It's a hidden reality, but hidden only by the limitations of our perception. With a little thought, a little imagination, and a willingness to see with fresh and open eyes (what another Buddhist teacher, Shunryu Suzuki, calls "beginner's mind"), suddenly interbeing is impossible to miss. And when we truly see how interconnected all beings are, it changes how we understand and relate to the world.

You might call this a mystical understanding of the universe. In this book, the words *mystic, mystical,* and *mysticism* show up repeatedly, so they deserve some commentary now. In a sense, these are terrible words because they get used by different people in so many different ways that they are practically useless. It's as if you drew a figure eight at a forty-five-degree angle so nobody could figure out if you meant to refer to infinity or simply the number after seven. Mysticism and its related words have, over the years, developed a similar ambiguity of meaning. And because mysticism often is associated with a kind of exotic spirituality, it gets lumped together with magic and miracles in a kind of alliterative trifecta of the supernatural.

But if we look at the Greek roots from which mysticism and its related words emerge, we meet a much more humble origin: more like 8 than ∞. Mysticism shares the same root that gives us the word *mystery*. This Greek word μυέω, *mueo*, refers to shutting or closing, like shutting your mouth or closing your eyes. It carries a sense of hiddenness, interiority, and ineffability—something that cannot be put into words.

In the Hebrew Bible, the prophet Isaiah is recorded as praying, "Truly, you are a God who hides himself" (Isaiah 45:15). The divine hiddenness or invisibility is one of God's most salient features. If you want to see the pope or the queen of England, you can; it might not be easy, since they are not the most accessible of folks, but they *can* be seen, on television if not in person. With God, there's no such luck. God remains hidden.

Yet what the mystics have been saying for centuries now is that God is hidden in plain sight—if we only could learn how to see ordinary things in an extraordinary way. Or just learn to see in a new way, from a new perspective. If we can learn to find infinity every time we look at the number eight, then—like William Blake—we can discern heaven in a flower or eternity in an hour. Which brings us back to our difficult word, *mysticism*.

Mysticism includes that dimension of spirituality that teaches us how to see, or know, or even imagine the hidden God and the hidden ways of God. A mystic, therefore, is simply a person who has embraced this new way of seeing, this mystical dimension of spirituality.

We can open up these words and find a lot more inside of them, like finding infinity inside the number eight (or entering Doctor Who's TARDIS, bigger on the inside than on the outside). Mystical spirituality invites us to discover a hidden life of meaning, purpose, spiritual consciousness, and joy. Mystics great and small, famous and obscure, have testified to this hidden life for centuries now. Each mystic seems to have charted their own course through the wilderness. But even so, there is some basic commonality to the roads they follow, so learning from them, on our own pilgrimage, we can find the landmarks and avoid the pitfalls as we make our own way.

Why listen to the mystics? Many of them were poets and philosophers whose writings could often be frustratingly dense or filled with an endless series of paradoxes and unfathomable symbolism. Yet their words, puzzling as they may be, invite us to examine the inscrutable mysteries of life itself. We can choose to live in an unreflective way, always a slave to our appetites, prone to addiction, and easily manipulated by people who want to make money off of us. Or we can get angry and rebellious and lose ourselves in cynicism that can lead to bitterness or violence. We can try to conform to some sort of religious or political ideology in a fundamentalist or dogmatic way and then spend the rest of our lives attacking people who see things differently. If we're clever, we might give ourselves to the pursuit of something noble, like art or science, and devote our lives to creating something that is beautiful or useful. And if our hearts are big enough, we might even lose ourselves in helping others, being of service in alleviating the suffering of the world.

We might, finally, choose to consider what the mystics offer us, learning to see with beginner's eyes and from new perspectives, opening our hearts to imagine the possibility that life just might have to do with something a whole lot bigger than us, something mysterious and hidden even as we see it showing up in moments of transcendent love, profound compassion, unexpected kindness or mercy, and inexplicable delight.

The mystics have called this possibility—and the life that it calls us to—by different names: enlightenment, ecstasy, nondual consciousness, union with God. That kind of elevated language has its place, but let's start in a more down-to-earth way by simply taking the mystical path seriously, understanding that it will lead us to joy. For a joyful life is a heavenly life, a life well lived.

Mysticism is generous: if you want to be an artist or a scientist while also pursuing the mystical life, you'll find there's plenty of room for both (or even all three).

Mystical spirituality goes so well with the life of service to others or advocacy for justice that they are
practically symbiotic: being in service to others and to
justice makes for a better mystic, and vice versa. And
the luminous, life-expansive way of the mystic will
beckon even the person lost in dogma or fundamental-
ism or addiction, although if you take the mystical life
seriously, sooner or later it will wean you away from
attempts to control or manage your life through rigid
systems of belief.

The mystical life invites us to see life from a new
perspective—that of infinite joy. To find this perspective, we need look no further than the treasury of blessings already hidden in our hearts. The path to joy is a
gift given to all of us. It is the first of a number of gifts
that we can find in our hearts. This isn't a new path,
but one celebrated by wisdom teachings found in many
traditions. One of those traditions is found in the Jewish
and Christian Scriptures. But this isn't just an invitation for Jews or Christians. These gifts are in all of our
hearts—just waiting to be recognized, acknowledged,
and celebrated.

When we find and embrace these gifts, imagine
how they can transform our lives and the lives of those
we touch. It's a transformation luminous with joy—and
a transformation I hope you'll discover for yourself.

Observant Christians and Jews regard their Bibles
as sacred Scripture. The sacred texts mean different

things to different people—some maintain the Bible contains no error; others see it as the work of human hands (errors, smudge marks, and all) that nevertheless offers a glimpse into the mind and heart of God. Not everyone automatically accepts the wisdom teaching and authority of those sacred texts—or, for that matter, the authority of other sacred texts, like the Qur'an or the Bhagavad Gita or the Dhammapada. But whether we are naturally believers or skeptics, it's helpful to approach a spiritual text like the Bible with an open mind but also a discerning heart. To see infinity in the number eight is a matter of perspective; likewise, finding mystical truth in an ancient sacred text might just require a willingness to consider what it has to say with an unprejudiced eye.

We read these sacred writings not just because somebody somewhere said these were holy books but because their own content marks them as classics of spiritual wisdom and insight.

I'm belaboring this point because *Eternal Heart* is organized around a series of gifts related to the heart, taken from the sacred writings of Hebrew and Christian Scripture. I'm aware some readers have a kind of automatic acceptance for anything in the Bible, while others take more of an "I'll believe it if it makes sense" approach.

Whatever your tradition or your view of biblical wisdom, I ask that you keep an open mind. See if these gifts of the heart can be inspirations to your imagination. Try to resist the urge to evaluate them strictly in terms of logic or reason. Receive these gifts with the wonder of a poet rather than the suspicion of a prosecutor—and then see where your heart takes you from there.

And while these gifts of the heart are the golden thread we will follow throughout our journey together, I'm also weaving in another wisdom teaching found in the Christian New Testament: the set of eight principles proclaimed by Jesus that are known as the Beatitudes, because each one begins with a blessing, "Blessed are" (in Latin, *Beati*). Each principle offers insight into how we can cultivate its blessing in our lives. The Greek word for "blessed," Μακάριοι, *makarioi*, also implies being happy or fortunate or even "living large." In other words, each of these beatitudes is also a step on the pathway to joy.

These eight beatitudes and eight blessings of the heart are woven together like strands of spiritual DNA. Each supports and amplifies the others and all call us forward to a life filled with hidden—that is to say, mystical—joy. As we recognize, honor, and cultivate these spiritual qualities and gifts and blessings, we open our hearts and minds and lives so that this hidden joy might truly manifest.

In the movie *Toy Story* and its various sequels, we meet a toy character named Buzz Lightyear, a space ranger action figure, who is known for his signature catchphrase: "To infinity . . . and beyond!" It's a bit of a joke: What can be beyond infinity, since infinity is by definition limitless?

Yet this notion existed even before our action figure gave it voice. Eli Maor, a historian of mathematics, wrote a book called *To Infinity and Beyond: A Cultural History of the Infinite*. Which makes me think, Why couldn't there be something beyond infinity? What's to stop the human imagination from poking into places that are beyond whatever limitlessness is?

It's just a rhetorical question. But I ask it because the imagination matters, as do questions that give our imagination room to play.

Let's imagine together. Let's imagine infinity and beyond. Let's imagine seeing things in a new way, and let's see what gifts await us, hidden in our very hearts. Then let's imagine how those gifts can make our lives better and help us create a better world. Finally, let's imagine how the gifts of the heart can take us beyond our wildest imagination—from our hearts to the very heart of mystery itself, the mystery of infinite love (what the mystics call God).

1

PASSAGE

"The divine presence is everywhere," proclaimed Saint Benedict some fifteen hundred years ago. We do not have to go anywhere to encounter the mystery called God.

The North African mystic, Saint Augustine, spoke the same truth in a different way. God, he said, is "more intimate than my interior and superior to my summit." His words, originally in Latin, could also be translated as "God is closer to me than I am to myself, and greater than I am at my best."

The divine presence is right here, inside each of us, both as we are and as we have the potential to become.

God doesn't stand still when we grow or move. God also doesn't run away when we rest.

Right here, right now, you dwell in the presence of the source of love, of life, of all being—the source of justice, of virtue, of all that makes life worth living. This includes, I might add, the source of all felicity, beatitude, and joy, but I do not want to get ahead of myself.

This teaching has roots all the way back in the Jewish Scriptures. One of the psalms declares, "Where can I go from your spirit? Or where can I flee from your presence? If I ascend to heaven, you are there; if I make my bed in Sheol [the underworld], you are there." In the Christian New Testament, the apostle Paul approvingly quotes a pagan poet: "In God we live and move and have our being." God is inside us; we are inside God. The divine presence is everywhere.

This isn't just a Jewish or Christian notion. The Qur'an points out that "to God belong the East and the West. Wheresoever you turn, there is the Face of God. God is All-Encompassing, Knowing" (surah 2:115).

The wisdom of the mystics throughout history echoes this teaching. "I saw that God is in all things," wrote the mediæval mystic Julian of Norwich. Two centuries later, Saint Ignatius of Loyola, in his beautiful meditation *Contemplation to Attain Love*, muses, "God dwells in creatures; in the elements; in the plants . . . in the animals . . . in human beings . . . God labors and works for me in all the creatures on the face of the earth." Later, in a letter, Ignatius expands this further. Spiritual seekers, he wrote, "should practice the seeking of God's presence in all things, in their conversations, their walks, in all that they see, taste, hear, understand in all their actions, since Divine Majesty is truly in all things by God's presence, power, and essence."

Now, a confession. I need to keep reminding myself of what Julian and Ignatius and Benedict and Augustine and all the rest say, over and over again. I need to keep reminding myself because I keep forgetting. I forget the divine presence is everywhere. I forget to seek God's presence in all things. I forget that wherever I turn, there is the face of God.

> I need to keep reminding myself because I keep forgetting. I forget the divine presence is everywhere. I forget to seek God's presence in all things. I forget that wherever I turn, there is the face of God.

Why is it so easy to forget that God is truly present? I think it goes back to the idea that God is hidden. We have to make our way through life, trusting in the reality of divine love and compassion, even if it feels like sometimes, we're lost in a fog. This reminds me of an experience I had on the Cumberland Plateau in Tennessee. This plateau stretches out west of the Cumberland Mountains, part of the Appalachian range. Where I lived on the plateau, in the college town of Sewanee, fog was a normal part of life. Usually it wasn't too bad. But once in a while, the fog would get truly dense—and dangerous—especially after sundown. More than once, I would be driving home as the fog rolled in. When the fog got thick enough, even dimmed headlights barely illuminated two or three feet ahead. The light got diffused and reflected off the waves of mist. Driving in dense fog is like driving in a blizzard. Long-term residents of "the mountain" offered advice on minimizing the risk. No matter how cold it is, they said, roll down the window to hear what's going on. And slow down—even if that meant driving through the fog at five miles per hour. They also taught me to train my eye on the reflecting line painted on the side of the road, since that was the only way to be sure you weren't driving off the pavement of that small-town, two-lane highway. Fortunately, I always got home safely—but it meant taking my time, moving forward slowly, being careful, and constantly paying attention.

Remembering to keep my eyes open for the hidden presence of God feels like the skill needed to drive through thick fog. It's about paying attention, listening carefully, and knowing when to slow down (or even to stop).

One of the great images for the mystery at the heart of the spiritual life is *the cloud of unknowing*, taken from the title of a fourteenth-century guide to contemplative prayer. I often think about the Sewanee fog when I think about the cloud of unknowing—conditions that are so dense, so thick, so lost in mist and darkness that a journey can only be taken one step at a time and requires paying close attention to nothing beyond where the next step leads. But when we learn to trust the divine presence hidden in the mist, we can move forward with confidence as well as care.

Like an encompassing band of fog, things cover our path, disorient us, throw us off our game, and challenge us in big and small ways. Health issues, financial setbacks, relationship problems, upsets at home or in the workplace, conflicts as small as a fight with a family member or as large as a nation at war. These life events that arise sometimes leave us feeling like we're just stumbling our way through the fog.

People deal with the challenges of life in many different ways, some healthier than others. To deal with the "fog" of life's challenges and setbacks, we might focus on orienting our lives toward accumulating money or power—strategies we might adopt in order to feel secure, or loved, or in control. Sometimes these strategies (what the Trappist monk Thomas Keating calls "programs for happiness") can be dysfunctional and can lead to alienation from others, to addiction, or even to situations where we are hurt by or hurt other people. Even at their best, the programs we build for happiness usually only offer us short-term benefits.

Augustine described the fact of our human condition—that we all seem to be travelers searching in a fog—as our *restless heart*. In his *Confessions*, he offers a prayer as profound as it is simple: "God, you have made us for yourself, and our hearts are restless until they rest in you."

When I forget the divine presence is everywhere, I feel like I'm lost in the fog. When life deals me challenges, again—lost in the fog. When everything, even life's blessings, ultimately fails to satisfy my restless heart, it feels like the angst of being lost in this "cloud of unknowing."

How can we allow our restless hearts to settle into the divine presence that seems so deeply hidden?

Here we encounter a paradox. If God is both truly present and yet also hidden, we have no choice but to seek that hidden God (even in the cloud). Such seeking implies a journey—a spiritual path to follow—but this journey seems to be one into a place where we already are. As the spiritual teacher Krishnamurti famously declared, "Truth is a pathless land."

Our lives are most certainly a journey of some sort, if only through time and place, but this spiritual journey, this pathless land, implies some sort of passage unlike any other. The mystics have compared it to climbing a mountain, exploring a castle, planting seeds, getting married, going on a pilgrimage, ascending a staircase, or simply just falling in love.

But journeys don't just spontaneously happen—at least, not most of the time. We go on a trip when somebody makes a decision. Maybe it's not always a trip we want (like going to the hospital or to court), but if we didn't make the choice, someone else did. Every trip begins with a *call* of some sort. The happiest ones are when the call emerges from within ourselves or from a loved one: "Hey, would you like to go to Ireland for our summer vacation?" But other calls can come from a neighbor, a business associate, a draft board, a dying parent, a spiritual teacher, a foundation, a rival. And spiritually speaking, a call can certainly come from God.

In fact, to the extent that *any* journey we take can be a spiritual journey, it's fair to look for God's hidden involvement whenever life (or someone) invites us on our next adventure. Since the divine presence is everywhere, God must be present, somehow, in every call.

One of the psalms in the Hebrew Bible says, "Happy are those whose strength is in you / in whose heart are the highways to Zion" (Psalm 84:5). On the surface, it appears that this psalm describes the happiness an observant Jew would find by making a pilgrimage to the sacred city of Jerusalem. But this thoroughfare that leads to spiritual happiness is not a physical road—but a highway *in the heart.*

As this psalm was written 2,500 years ago, the word *highway* does not mean the asphalt-covered, traffic-congested freeways of our time, dangerous to pedestrians and foul with the fumes of exhaust. Try to imagine something more earthy and organic—a pedestrian parkway, where anyone is welcome to travel; in the poetic words of Antonio Machado, "The path is made by walking."

Your heart may be restless in such a way that no earthly satisfaction can ever quell its desire. But the path to fulfilling that desire begins right there, in the center of your restless heart. This is the first gift of the heart: a pathway to all the other gifts.

One of the great masterpieces of Western spiritual literature is a small book, likely written by a Russian Orthodox monk in the 1800s, called *The Way of a Pilgrim*. It's a book about living a life immersed in prayer. The subject of this book is a wanderer. We often associate the word *pilgrim* with traveling for spiritual purposes, like going to Jerusalem or Lourdes or Mecca. But pilgrimage does not necessarily require a carefully planned itinerary. As spiritually motivated wandering, pilgrimage has a long history—such as Abraham, leaving his home to respond to God's call, or Ruth, the Moabite woman who travels with her mother-in-law, Naomi, in search of a better life.

The saints of the early Celtic lands saw pilgrimage as a holy act. It was a search for "the place of your resurrection," which is to say, the place where you will die—and someday be raised again. Not many people think in those terms now. We move somewhere to go to school or pursue a job opportunity. We don't see ourselves as settling down and establishing roots. We're just passing through. In that sense, the spiritual sense of pilgrimage has given way to a more rootless, perhaps even anxious, way of perceiving life as a self-interested journey.

Spiritually speaking, a pilgrimage might not even require a physical relocation. We might even embark upon a "pilgrimage of the heart"—an idea that makes sense, in light of the psalm, where the "highway" of our spiritual journey begins right in our hearts.

This first gift of the heart is its capacity for pilgrimage, whether physical or spiritual. Even if you live your entire life in one place (and there's something to be said for that), your heart may still be called to wander, in wonder. Responding to that call is the first step toward finding the hidden/present divine.

> **The path to fulfilling that desire begins right there, in the center of your restless heart. This is the first gift of the heart: a pathway to all the other gifts.**

Because the heart is restless, it will want to follow the highway within, wherever it may lead us—even through the fog and the cloud of unknowing, but always in search of the sacred rest that ultimately comes from the heart of God.

"Happy are those whose strength is in God—in their hearts are pilgrim's highways." I suppose you might read this psalm in a conditional way, as if the pilgrim's highway is not in everyone's heart but only in those who find their strength in God. But that would be to forget that *all* strength comes from the divine. God is love, the Spirit of life and compassion and mercy and forgiveness. We are all strengthened by love and life, even when we don't consciously comprehend that.

A highway is built so that it goes somewhere. A road always takes you from point A to point Z, with plenty of other points in between. Highways wander through town and country, over hills and across rivers, and they almost never follow a straight line. And even cared-for highways have hazards, construction zones, obstacles in the road.

As traveler-pilgrims on the "highway of life," we will meet others on the road. I might meet someone who tells me that the only way God will accept me is if I conform completely to their religious beliefs and customs. Or they might be agnostic or atheist or express spirituality in a manner quite unlike my own. They might not read the sacred texts the same way I do. It's not always easy to connect with those we encounter on the spiritual pathways of life, especially when they seem to be walking in a different direction or seeking a different destination.

But we're all on the road, going somewhere. The most interesting question is not "Where are you?" at this moment in time but "Where are you going?"

Is the highway that you're on leading toward a more compassionate, caring, people-centered life? Is it a road that goes toward hope, and wonder, and faith, and trust, and courage? Does this path you're on offer a sense of adventure, promising spiritual growth, beautiful vistas, and the opportunity to share your blessings with others—or does it seem to be more like a cul-de-sac, or maybe just a closed-circuit raceway where you literally just keep going around in circles?

From the annals of myth and legend and history, we know heroic journeys are rarely free of peril. If we don't have a very good map, or if we entrust ourselves to an unreliable guide, we could easily get lost—even go the wrong way. We can get thrown off course by any of the hazards we encounter along the way. We might take a wrong turn and get lost in the forest. All sorts of problems can beset our journey.

There are so many ways we can get lost along our pilgrim's highway. We might get ensnared by addiction or trade away happiness for financial or emotional security. We may lack the skills necessary to communicate well or manage conflict, which can lead to an unhappy marriage or a string of failed relationships. We can choose to frame our lives with cynicism or bitterness, allowing fear or resentment to shape our worldview and leach away our peace of mind. And sometimes our lives veer off course for reasons totally beyond our control—our company gets sold and we lose our job or our life gets shattered by an unexpected illness, loss, or betrayal. If you have not known scenarios like these in your life, you probably know of people who have.

Looking back on my own life, I see all sorts of bad turns, missed byways, and unfortunate twists of fate that complicated my life's pilgrimage. Some of them were of my own choosing. Others involved forces outside of my control. But no matter how dire the circumstances might have been, I always had the opportunity to travel a little bit further on the highway of my life journey. There's always the hope that tomorrow will bring a better day. Even when we have traveled far down life's road, we can always make choices to foster more love, or peace, or happiness, or healing.

Like the highway of life, the pathway in our hearts beckons us toward an interior adventure. The great spiritual teachers of the world offer the image of a path when describing the process of attaining spiritual maturity, or enlightenment, or wisdom, or holiness. John of the Cross described the mystical life as "the ascent of Mount Carmel," based on the idea that this ancient mountain located in Israel was the place where Elijah encountered the presence of God. You and I may never make it to the Holy Land, physically speaking, yet the pathway of our hearts can take us up to that interior mountaintop where we can just as assuredly encounter the presence of God.

The beauty of the heart highway is that, even with making mistakes or taking wrong turns or getting mired in a roadside hazard, there's always a chance to get back on course. The much-maligned religious word *repentance* literally means "to adopt a new consciousness." It also carries the connotation of "to change the road you're on." I saw a bumper sticker once that whimsically put it, "God Allows U-Turns!" God does give us every opportunity to overcome the obstacles, get off the roundabout, and return to the heart pathway toward living an authentic life, a true life, and indeed, a good life—a life marked by love, contentment, and happiness.

All of us are pilgrims, wanderers, travelers. But our lives sometimes seem to be shaped by anything but love, happiness, and contentment. As Thoreau put it, "The mass of men lead lives of quiet desperation." Systems of economic inequality, racism, sexism, homophobia, transphobia, barriers to those who are handicapped or struggle with mental illness—the reasons are legion for why many find life more filled with "quiet desperation" than "love, joy, peace."

Does it have to be this way? I hope not. But if we're going to talk about the destination of the heart's highway, we also need to acknowledge that sometimes, where we're coming from—or where we currently are—may not look anything like where we hope to arrive. Our challenge in those times of "quiet desperation" is to make sure we avoid the temptation to turn to cynicism or apathy—perspectives shaped by a feeling that there's no point or no hope. As long as we can remember that we are on the highway, and the journey is not yet ended, we can foster hope even in the most trying of times.

The path is always there, and it leads somewhere.

And on this path, we're called to be seekers, to believe in the dream, and to take that all-important first step (or next step). Julian of Norwich, whose life had its own measure of difficulties (she lived through the time of plague in the Middle Ages), understood that there are two basic types of prayer: "seeking" and "beholding."

The prayer of *beholding* is infinitely beautiful, giving us a profound sense of God's presence in our lives, a sense of blessing and felicity that comes through union with the divine. As a realist, Julian also recognized that many people rarely (or never) have such an exalted experience of prayer. For most of us, prayer is marked more by *seeking*—a longing or yearning for the divine presence we do not seem to have. It's the prayer of being lost in the fog or mired in the cloud of unknowing. If you aren't at your hoped-for destination, it's not the end of the world—but it *is* time to get moving.

The New Testament offers a wonderful insight into love's source: "We love, because God first loved us." It also compares the Spirit of love to a widow earnestly seeking to find a lost coin—persistent and dogged. Combine these aspects, and a powerful principle emerges: we seek the face of divine love because divine love is seeking us.

Our seeking emerges within our hearts because our hearts are attuned to love seeking us. Anytime you recognize the restlessness in your heart that Augustine speaks of, your heart is resonating with the divine presence that is closer to you than you are to yourself. God calls you to seek God—to seek love, hope, faith, peace, and joy.

> On this path, we're called to be seekers, to believe in the dream, and to take that all-important first step (or next step).

Julian describes three steps to such seeking:

1. A willingness to be a seeker
2. The faith to start the journey
3. Trust that the road actually leads somewhere

At the beginning of his Sermon on the Mount, Jesus offers eight beatitudes—gnomic wisdom teachings that link blessedness or happiness to specific choices we can make, or virtues we cultivate in our lives. On our journey toward finding the divine presence in our hearts, these beatitudes function as helpful landmarks along the highway. Let's lead off with the beatitude that points toward the goal of every restless heart: to see God. Jesus says, "Blessed are the pure in heart, for they will see God" (Matthew 5:8).

Over the centuries, *purity* has been used for religious and political control. It can be a dangerous concept— used to justify genocide like the Shoah (Holocaust) as well as a code word for controlling people's sexual behavior. But the word Jesus uses—the Greek word καθαροὶ, *katharoi*—carries a different meaning. *Katharoi* is a root of the word *catharsis*. Catharsis, in the annals of Western mysticism, is the necessary first step on the journey toward union with God. Here *pure* not only suggests a freedom from contaminating elements; it also could simply be rendered as *clean*. We might rephrase the beatitude as "Blessed is a free and cleansed heart, for it shall see God."

"Seeing God" doesn't happen automatically. The God of love is gentle and not willing to force the divine presence on those who just don't want it. Most of us are a paradox: we want it, and we don't want it. We have mixed hearts, hearts that know the only true rest is in God but nevertheless remain invested in all sorts of other pleasures—some perfectly benign and others not so good. With this reality in mind, it's important to read Jesus's beatitude as a challenge as well as an invitation—not as an accusation or a shaming.

Jesus knows that no human being has a perfectly clean (pure) heart. But in his wisdom, he's asking, "Are you willing to show up? Are you willing to do the work? Are you willing to clean up your mess?" To answer yes to these questions is to commit to the path. We see this echoed in the wisdom teachings of Julian of Norwich: make the commitment, have faith, and trust. And do it with gladness and delight. There's the cleansing right there. Are we willing to begin to let go of gratuitous cynicism, nursed resentments, dispiriting bitterness, and the kind of negativity that leaches away our energy and gives us nothing in return? Letting go of those kinds of afflictive thoughts launches us on the journey of catharsis, of inner cleansing, that prepares us to receive the presence of the One who is already there.

Julian encourages us to have faith. That's not always easy. Our society rewards pessimism and suspicion and all too often rejects faith or faithfulness as a kind of naive escape into fantasy. But just because that's the default perspective in our world does not mean we have to settle for it. The way of faith (of hope, of optimism, of trust) and the way of cynicism (of suspicion, of nihilism, of endless doubt) are like two lenses that we can wear in order to see the world. One lens filters out all that is discouraging; the other filters out all that is hopeful. Our eyes, especially at first, are not capable of seeing the entire spectrum, so we have to start somewhere. The lens of faith will eventually strengthen our eyes to the point where we can begin to take an honest, hard look at those places in our hearts where cynicism and discouragement reside. In other words, faith eventually gives us the strength for inner healing. But the lens of doubt works differently. It just leads to more pessimism, more cynicism, more despondency. It never makes room for the way of faith—and it never functions in a self-corrective way.

For many, faith may seem simply unattainable—or worse, a kind of intellectual suicide that replaces reason with magical thinking. We talk about a "leap of faith"—this implies we can never think or reason our way to a place of true faith; sooner or later, we have to make a trusting dive into the unknown. How, then, can we find faith? There's a reason Julian did not lead off with faith: she began with an invitation to intentionality. The apostle Paul describes faithfulness as a fruit of the Spirit in his letter to the Galatians (5:22–23)—a sign of the Spirit's presence in our lives. It follows that faith itself is a gift, given to the heart that truly seeks it. Faith is not something we can just decide to do, like turning on a light switch. Rather, it is a fruit, gradually grown in a life continually nurtured by remaining open to and continually seeking divine love and the divine presence.

If you feel like faith is simply not a part of your life, or if it's hard for you to imagine trusting in God (or in Love), please keep your heart open—and resist cynicism. Consider the gift of faith as something given to you slowly over time. It's something you will find gradually. To manifest faith, you begin in the dark and slowly walk toward, and into, the dawn. Allow faith to take time to grow in your restless heart. Remember, the first step is simply making the commitment to walk the path that has been given to you in your heart. The gifts you will need to make your journey flourish will become apparent along the way.

The Buddhist teacher Pema Chödrön wrote a book with a title that sums up this stage on the journey: *Start Where You Are*. We may wish we were somewhere else in life, but the plain truth is, we are where we are. The pathway in our hearts is a promise from God that we don't have to stay anywhere that brings us misery or suffering. Leaving that place might entail a physical relocation, a spiritual transformation, or even simply learning new skills to deal with what's in front of us. Everyone's life is unique, and so too is everyone's journey. Pema Chödrön talks about "awakening the heart" as an essential step on the spiritual path. She cites a Buddhist slogan, "All activities should be done with one intention," and that one intention, as she interprets it, is awakening the heart. She speaks of *bodhicitta*, a Sanskrit word that means "enlightened consciousness." An awakened heart is a conscious heart—a heart that knows its own restlessness and seeks the path of love, of compassion, of enlightenment. For those of us who follow the teachings of the Western mystics, we would add that such an awakened heart seeks the presence of God, trusting that only in God will it find ultimate rest.

Some people associate consciousness or enlightenment with the mind rather than the heart. But I invite you to imagine that the heart may have more to do with consciousness and enlightenment than we have traditionally understood or recognized—a theme we will return to as we continue along this path.

Heart Practice:
Prayer as Longing, Longing as Prayer

So how do we begin? How do we find that path of the heart that can lead us through our innate restlessness to the place we long to go—the place of happiness, of beatitude and felicity, of enlightenment and the divine presence? In the Western spiritual tradition, there are only a handful of essential spiritual practices, and we will consider each of them in turn as we take this journey together. What all these spiritual practices have in common is that they are all forms of prayer. Prayer, then, is the place to begin.

People define prayer in different ways, but at its most basic, we might think of it simply as responding to God. We can do this with words (saying prayers) or with actions (pray with your feet); we can pray out loud or in the silence of our hearts. We can pray by cultivating trust in God and compassion in others and then living accordingly. Even adopting a particular consciousness, such as a nondual awareness where we recognize the interconnectedness of all things, may be a way of praying.

Prayer is related to noticing. If we notice what's going on in our hearts and minds, we are more likely to respond consciously and intentionally, making skillful choices that move us farther along our path. We cannot *make* God present in our hearts; as the mystics remind us, the divine presence is everywhere. We do not cause God to be present, but we can learn to notice the One who is there.

Granted, the divine presence doesn't always seem very noticeable. We seek God, and all we find is our longing, our restlessness, our yearning. That's a start. Remember: start where you are. Begin your journey of prayer by simply observing who you are and where you are. Notice your body. How does it feel? How comfortable are you as an embodied person? Do you feel restless and anxious, sad and discouraged, bitter and angry, or excited and ungrounded? Don't judge, just pay attention. Let the noticing be a prayer. By perceiving what's going on in your heart and mind and body, you are praying—sharing yourself with God. And perhaps in that sharing, you will discern the face of God.

Whatever you notice, whatever arises, let that be your prayer. Pay special attention to your longings. Are you longing for comfort, for peace, for love? Are you restless for happiness, a sense of meaning, a sense of hope? Is your heart crying for guidance, yearning for a sense of God's presence? Take time to observe where the yearning, the longing, the disquiet is in your heart. It's there somewhere. We all have it: it's part of the human condition.

As you begin to notice your restlessness, you may feel a desire to frame your restlessness with words: "God, here I am, in my messy restless glory" or "God, I'm not even sure I believe in you, but I do know I have a restless heart, and I'm willing to let this yearning be a bridge to you." Praying verbally is not an essential part of this practice, but if the words come, let them. Simply notice what does or doesn't arise.

Finally, try to see your restlessness and longing from different perspectives. See them not just as formless feelings gurgling within your heart but rather as the raw energy of *seeking*—the fuel that will propel you along the pathway in your heart. Try to see the restlessness as a resource, a turbine that will give you all you need to begin and persevere in the journey from your heart to the heart of God. If a turbine is too mechanical a metaphor for you, simply bring it back into your body: the restlessness is the kinetic energy that gives your muscles the vitality they need to live well, including the muscle of your heart. Your physical heart is a muscle, a pump that keeps you alive. Likewise, your spiritual heart is a "spiritual muscle" that can and will cooperate with the Spirit of God to guide you into the temple of joy. Trust the energy of your restless longing, trust that this energy can be framed as the prayer of seeking, and move forward into the adventure of your life, walking along the highway given to you in your heart.

2

SILENCE

When I was a child, perhaps nine or ten years old, my mother arranged for me to attend an arts program at a local junior high school. It took place on a Saturday—in the summertime, I believe. The gymnasium at the school had been repurposed as a giant art studio, where kids from all over the city could come and spend the day being creative. Throughout the gym, various workstations were set up where we could play with paints, crayons, colored pencils, or various items for creating pictures or collages or even small three-dimensional masterpieces, glued together as our artistic imaginations directed us.

Many years have spun by since then, and I only have fleeting memories of whatever it was I created. But my heart sings whenever I think of that Saturday. It was as if I stepped out of the normal flow of time, even if for just a while. I got lost in the eternal now of creative being, letting my timid inner artist come out to play.

I don't know how long this event lasted—probably only a couple of hours. But time seemed to stand still, as if each moment just opened up into eternity. When the program ended and Mom came to the school to collect me, I happily shared all of my creations with her. I don't know whatever became of my handiwork, but that's hardly what matters. I had been invited into a sacred time and special place where the point was not to be productive or to measure up to someone else's benchmark but rather simply to inhabit that place in my heart where imagination, playfulness, and creativity dance. I did not grow up to be an artist, but perhaps my vocation as a writer was somehow encouraged that day—for we have many different ways to be creative. Indeed, all artistry and creativity begin in what has been called the *imaginal* space—an interior dimension where inspiration, inner vision, and creative impulse dance together in a circle of delight and possibility.

Going to that gymnasium on that summer Saturday represented a sacred pause, a moment of time opening up that allowed me, just for a day, to try being someone else, someone different from however my ordinary day-to-day circumstances had been shaped. And because I entered into that pause and allowed myself to explore new possibilities, I was changed forever.

Such a pause—stepping away from the hurly-burly of work and the fast pace of an active life—is like taking a moment for rest and reflection, for generative stillness. Who knows what possibilities our imaginal minds (and hearts) will come up with?

One of the most beloved of Jesus's sayings is "Come to me, all you that are weary and are carrying heavy burdens, and I will give you rest" (Matthew 11:28). We might read these words in a general sense, but it's easy to see how this gift he promises us is, among other things, a gift of the heart. A busy working heart carries the burdens of the body: A typical healthy heart beats, on average, 80 beats a minute (60 beats while resting, 100 beats or more while active). That translates to 4,800 beats an hour, 115,200 beats each day, and over 42 *million* beats each year. Based on the global life expectancy of seventy-two years, that works out to more than 3 *billion* heartbeats over the course of a typical life span.

After every single one of those three billion heartbeats, your heart takes a rest. After every contraction of cardiac muscle that sends blood coursing throughout the body—first to your lungs to gather needed oxygen and then to every part of you to distribute nutrients and gather up waste—your heart takes a rest. It may only be for a fraction of a second, but in that tiny moment, your heart is silent. Then another beat, and another rest, and so on it goes for billions of moments over all the days of your life.

The Cloud of Unknowing maintains that all human beings are accountable for every "atom" of time we have been given (in our day, we think of an atom as one of the smallest particles of matter, but in the fourteenth century, *The Cloud* uses that word to mean the smallest unit of time, what we might now call a nanosecond). Call it an atom or a nanosecond or the pause between heartbeats, every minuscule moment of time is a gift given to us, and we are invited to use that gift wisely. Every instant of time deserves to be received and used conscientiously. Our hearts may be pounding away at 130 beats per minute (say, right after a workout or upon learning that someone truly loves you), but every tiny moment of rest between each pulse remains a gift given.

What if that silent pause—that rest—were a gift in our hearts? One Scripture verse hints that this is so. Peter's first letter has this to say about the importance of inner beauty: "Let your adornment be the inner self with the lasting beauty of a gentle and quiet spirit, which is very precious in God's sight" (1 Peter 3:4). In the original Greek, the word used for "inner self" is καρδίας, *kardias*, "the human heart." We all have within us a "gentle and quiet spirit" in our hearts—both in the rest between the beats and beyond. And the word translated as "quiet" in the original Greek is ἡσυχίου, *hesychiou,* a rich word that means not only "silence" but "contemplative silence"—the silence of the mystics. That's the kind of silence that has been given to us in our hearts.

Like the silence between them, the heartbeats themselves are also gifts. Our first heartbeat emerges from silence, and then at the moment of death, the final beat yields itself into the silence of eternity. Thus every single heartbeat over the course of a life span is embraced by silence. The gift of silence is there before the beginning and remains even beyond the end. Silence is the chalice that holds the wine of our hearts' pulsing efforts.

Life is lived with, and in between, every heartbeat. Just as silence fills the space between each pulse, so silence rests between every thought we think. For some of us, it may be easier to access the silence in the heart even more than the silence in the mind.

After every single one of those heartbeats— 42 million beats of your heart per year—your heart takes a rest. After every contraction of cardiac muscle that sends blood coursing throughout the body—your heart takes a rest. It may only be for a fraction of a second, but in that tiny moment, your heart is silent. Then another beat, and another rest, and so on over all the days of your life.

Eastern Orthodox Christians practice the "Prayer of the Heart," a method of deep prayer in which, through repeatedly reciting the name of Jesus (or the Jesus

Prayer), you enable your mind to *sink into* your heart. This may seem confusing. But in an imaginal way, your mind sinks into your heart when you allow the drumming rhythm of your heartbeat—followed by the gracious abyss of silence, no matter how momentary—to caress and embrace the normal frenzy of thought after thought that comprises the ordinary consciousness of the egoic mind. It is only in the loving embrace of the heart, with its alternating gifts of the beat of life and the vastness of silence, that the mind can find *its* way into recognizing, however momentary, the spaciousness that already exists between all our thoughts. We often ignore the silence within us, which is to say, we often ignore the very language of God in our hearts. We walk the path of the eternal heart to seek solace for our interior disquiet. To find the calm in our restless hearts, we simply need to attend to that silence already beneath and between every beat.

"Silence is God's first language; everything else is a poor translation." These words come from Thomas Keating, though they sound like something Rumi or any of numerous other contemplative teachers from over the ages could have said. To listen to silence means to listen to the wordless voice of God—wordless not because God is inchoate or incoherent but because God communicates with us at a place too deep for words. And we have direct access to that place through two centers of awareness in our bodies: the mind and the heart. And as the Orthodox tradition teaches, the most effective way to pray, to receive that voice of God, is imaginally to place our minds in our hearts.

The human family enjoys a diversity of languages, stories, cultures, religions, philosophies, and wisdom traditions. Beneath them all, there is only one silence. The silence in our hearts is the same silence in our minds and in our souls. In silence we may find the rest Christ promised us.

We may feel our hearts beating, and we may obsess over the endless array of thoughts, the so-called stream of consciousness, but too often we forget to notice the silence—God's first language—beneath and between every thought and every heartbeat. When we gaze beyond the noise to find the silence, we find it is always already there, just awaiting our attention.

The silence—the stillness and the rest in our hearts— matters because it functions as the threshold to the wisdom deep in our hearts that cannot be put into words—wisdom that comes from and leads to God. Such silent wisdom opens us up to the imaginal world, that place within us filled with infinite possibility, a mystical place available to all of us in our hearts. We can pass our days without ever noticing, let alone crossing, this threshold. This is why times of rest, times of retreat, times of "pause" matter so much. They are opportunities for us to discover (or rediscover) that the threshold into silence, into the imaginal realm, is within us. We simply have to accept the heart's invitation and embrace that luminous, silent space.

A spiritual virtue that enables us to cross the threshold into the place where rest and silence meet is humility. Not humiliation, or self-abnegation, or self-contempt. Sacred humility is simply being down to earth, being ourselves. It may even seem a bit self-forgetful, a letting go of the need to be focused on ourselves, which often amounts to just being obsessed with the ever-changing drama of our egos.

Christ affirms the spiritual wisdom of humility in one of the Beatitudes: "Blessed are the meek, for they shall inherit the earth" (Matthew 5:5). The Greek word πραεῖς, *praeis*, loses some of its meaning when translated into English. Our word *meek* has a sense of being mousy or weak. *Praeis* comes from *praus*, a Greek root that implies "gentle strength." Meekness comes not from being weak but from knowing how true strength has a quality of tenderness and mildness—it is a heart-centered, compassionate strength rather than the more brittle kind of strength that sees everything in a dualistic way, as though power and weakness were binaries. Jesus proclaims that beatific happiness is a manifestation of humble strength—meekness that knows how to temper power with gentleness. As for inheriting the earth, it is a mutual, communal inheritance, just as when a family elder passes away and their wealth is shared among all the children and grandchildren. So those who are humble and gently strong not only receive a gift of blessed delight but, thanks to their humility, freely share this beatitude with others.

This self-forgetful, gentle/strong meekness is the humility that guides us to and through the threshold of silence, allowing us to be receptive and open to the whisper of eternity deep in our hearts, the still small voice that is more silent than silence itself.

In order to cultivate this gentle strength, we begin by offering a gesture of consent, of longing, of desire to manifest this and other drawing-to-God qualities that bring restlessness "home." The answer rests within our hearts. Every heartbeat is a show of strength, a burst of energy that acclaims "yes" to life. Then after every heartbeat comes the moment, however minuscule, of silent rest.

Strength, then gentleness.

Action, then contemplation.

We cultivate the humble heart not by what we do but by who we realize we are. We are stardust, creations of a loving God. We are the custodians of billions of heartbeats cradled in the eternity of silence.

> **Times of rest, times of retreat, times of "pause" matter. They are opportunities for us to discover (or rediscover) that the threshold into silence, into the imaginal realm, is within us.**

And sometimes, it's gentleness that precedes strength. Contemplation, then action—the yielding, the silence, the listening, the wondering before the decisive action, effort, or show of strength. After all, silence precedes every heartbeat as surely as it follows each pulse.

Strength—real strength, the strength of the Spirit— emerges out of gentleness, and not the other way around. When we recognize the silence in our hearts, a gift given from before the beginning of time by a Spirit who loves us, we make it possible for that same Spirit to increase the meek, gentle strength within us—the strength that empowers us to inherit and share the earth.

When I think about that magical day creating art when I was a boy, I think about gentleness and strength. Creativity requires both. We need strength because it takes courage to create—boldness to make a statement using color, or sound, or language, or dance. Every artist must grapple with the notion that his or her work might be a failure, might be met with derision or disdain, or worse yet, might be simply ignored by others. To be creative requires inner strength more than brute strength (although, to be fair, some art—like Michelangelo's *David*—probably required a fair amount of muscle as well). And then, our capacity to create requires more than just power and daring: art emerges out of that place within us that is contemplative, listening as well as speaking, wondering at possibilities before deciding on a particular course of action. Perhaps this is why many artists speak about dreams or even talk of being inspired in a dream. One such example is the melody to "Yesterday," perhaps the most famous song ever performed by the Beatles, which originally came to Paul McCartney in a dream. We need receptivity to create as surely as we need the inner strength to do so.

I know a Trappist monk who insists that the unconscious believes everything it is told. He says he read this somewhere, that it's a matter of psychological science, even though he can't point me to the source of the research. Still, I find myself intuitively nodding. We can use our imagination to "create" realities that our unconscious minds (and our hearts) will calibrate themselves around. Imagine a world filled with hope and possibility, and you will begin in subtle ways to create that world, even if just in your own life.

Imagine a world where love is abundant, and you will begin to relate to others out of that sense that there is plenty of love to go around. Has your imagination created this love, this trust, this hope? I don't know. Maybe it all comes from God, but the imagination allows your heart to receive—and share—all the blessings that you imagine to be possible.

"Who but you can see in the dark of a heart?" asked the poet Mirabai. Her poems dance with bhakti (devotion) to the unseen one who nevertheless can see even into the silence between our heartbeats. The idea of a "dark heart" may seem ominous to some, suggesting a heart that has turned away from the light of God. But I do not think that was Mirabai's meaning. For even a saintly heart is dark in the sense of being hidden, secluded, or shrouded in mystery.

Isaiah the prophet proclaimed to God, "Truly, you are a God who hides" (Isaiah 45:15), and more than one mystic has quite sensibly described this hiddenness of God in terms of divine darkness—or, for that matter, divine silence. This silent hiddenness is the cloud of unknowing. So as God is hidden behind the cloud, so too is the human heart. It is not only physically hidden, buried deep in the chest, but spiritually hidden as well, for no one can access our hearts but ourselves and God.

Perhaps Mirabai's point is that our "dark hearts" remain hidden even to ourselves. Jeremiah the prophet spoke dourly of how deceitful the human heart can be—we'll take a closer look at this as we go farther down the path. Our words and even our behaviors can deceive another person, whereas our hearts can deceive even ourselves. This deception can lead to decisions and commitments that have long-lasting, perhaps lifelong, consequences. All the more reason to turn to the One who gives us the silence in our hearts, that we might make our hearts available to the divine gaze—entering into a *being-known* in a manner greater than we even know ourselves.

The heart is mentioned about forty times in *The Cloud of Unknowing*. Its anonymous author accepts the idea that the head governs thought, logic, and reason, while the heart governs intuition, emotion, and feeling. This is a common understanding in our society, yet the relationship between thought and emotion, or between reason and intuition, is far more intimate than any kind of perceived split between head and heart suggests. We developed this perspective because it helps us make sense of what it means to be human: some of us are thinkers, and others are feelers. To the author of *The Cloud of Unknowing*, there's no contest as to which aspect of the human experience is better suited for fostering intimacy with God.

"Of God himself can no person think," declares the author of *The Cloud*. "For God may well be loved, but not thought. By love may God be 'gotten' and held, but by thought, never." Someone once said that a God small enough to be comprehended by the mind is a God too small to worship. Most mystics would agree. According to *The Cloud of Unknowing*, where the thinking, rational mind falls short, the power of love remains our one possibility for truly touching, and embracing, the divine presence.

What we cannot wrap our minds around, our hearts may truly embrace. The power that makes this possible is the power of love—and the silence within us, for "like speaks to like," and the silence between the pulsations of a beating heart comes from, and returns to, the silence that is God's first language.

Heart Practice:
Entering Meditative, Imaginal Space

The Cloud of Unknowing promotes a radical immersion into silence—God's silence and our own. Such a silent way of prayer will be important and meaningful all along the path of the heart. For now, still so close to the beginning of our pilgrimage, I want to commend a different invitation into prayer—one related to the spiritual exercises of Ignatius of Loyola. We can call this imaginative meditation or simply imaginative prayer.

Imagination is a luminous gift from God. "What is now proved was once, only imagined," wrote William Blake, pointing out how all that exists, once upon a time, first emerged in imaginal space—if not in someone's earthly imagination, then in the imagination of God.

In his song about an Anne Sexton poem, "Mercy Street," Peter Gabriel muses on how all things made by human hands begin first as a dream inside someone's head. Michelangelo had to imagine the Sistine Chapel before he could paint it; Alice Walker had to imagine the story of Celie before she wrote *The Color Purple*. Einstein supposedly claimed, "Imagination is more important than knowledge"—or words to that effect. The basic idea is sound: all that exists originated somewhere in the imagination. This means, of course, that when we use our imaginations, we step into creative possibility. We can invest our energy, our ideas, our creative dreams and visions and hopes into imagining what we wish might be.

Granted, many imaginings never go beyond idle daydreams, and some imagined things (like violence or chaotic destruction) ought to remain unreal. But in the context of prayer, we can imagine what may be possible and invest it with faith and hope and creative energy, which creates the room in our hearts for the Holy Spirit to act, making tomorrow's reality out of today's potentiality.

I invite you to pray in an imaginative, creative way, and to do so with both a sense of playful possibility and an earnest commitment to imagining with love—which includes justice, responsibility, and care. When I pray, I can imagine blessings as though they were rose petals pouring forth on those I love. I can imagine healing for the sick, comfort for the sorrowful, peace for the anxious, trust for the fearful, and companionship for the lonely. I can imagine all the ways God calls me to be a blessing in the world. I can imagine a world where people work together to foster peace and justice— to dismantle racism, sexism, homophobia, and other forms of systemic oppression—and where equality and inclusivity are both celebrated and protected. Most of all, I can imagine feeling and experiencing and truly knowing God's love and care for me and all others. I can imagine God's presence in my heart, giving me all the gifts I need to live my life with meaning and purpose.

> **But what thought can never accomplish in prayer, love makes possible.**

If I am unhappy, I can imagine God bringing me peace.

If I am agitated, I can imagine finding rest in God.

If I am suffering, I can imagine the ways God can bring me comfort and succor.

To practice prayer-as-imagination and imagination-as-prayer, give yourself the gift of spending some time each day in an exercise of guided daydreaming with God. Imagine what it would be like to truly manifest the fullness of God's love and light and felicity in your heart—and your life. Imagine how God's presence in your heart can transform your life from the inside out. Imagine the difference you can make in your community if you begin living out of that place where you touch God through silence and love, trusting that the divine presence is within you, even if you can't feel it. Because even if you can't feel it, you can imagine it. And if you can imagine it, you are opening your heart to it, regardless of what you may think about it. God, God's mystery, and God's love all come into our lives at a level that is beyond the capacity of our mental cognition. But what thought can never accomplish in prayer, love makes possible. Love—acting with creativity, resting in silence, and acting with faith and hope—is the raw energy of manifesting a joyful life. Imagine God pouring God's love into you and through you to others. Allow this imagination to shape your prayer, and just as every moment of rest precedes a new heartbeat, imagine how your prayer can lead you to creative action. Then, make it so.

3

DISCERNMENT

I have a wonderful relationship with a community called the Worker Sisters and Brothers of the Holy Spirit. Rooted in the Episcopal Church yet ecumenical in scope, they are a covenanted group of women and men—single and married, lay and ordained—who commit to a common life of faith in Christ, following the spirituality and teachings found in *The Rule of Saint Benedict*.

Over the years, I've led several retreats for the community on topics ranging from Celtic spirituality to the Beatitudes. One year, the community's prioress, Sr. LaVerne Peter, WSHS, asked me if I could develop a retreat on the topic of understanding Jesus in his Jewish context. I agreed, knowing that one of the many blind spots within Christianity is a lack of knowledge about and appreciation for how first-century Jewish culture, identity, and spirituality shaped Jesus and his message as well as the lives of the earliest Christians.

As I prepared for the retreat, reading Jewish scholars like Amy-Jill Levine, Abraham Joshua Heschel, and Lawrence Kushner gave me not only a profound insight into the religious background of Jesus and his message but also a deep appreciation for Judaism as it exists today. It was also sobering and humbling to discover how many subtle anti-Jewish and anti-Semitic ideas continue to shape Christianity.

From Sabbath customs, to dietary restrictions, to purity codes, Christianity's perception of the Jewish law (also known as Torah) often seems to be based on a perception of the law as rigid, lifeless, perfectionistic—referencing it as the "tyranny" of Jewish law. The more I learned about Judaism, the more I discovered that Christian ideas about the Torah were sometimes wildly inaccurate and that Judaism offered a much richer and more nuanced way to think about God's law. For Jews, the law is a source of life: the Torah represents the very mind of God rendered in written form for us to study, learn from, and celebrate.

Nowhere is this more clearly brought home than in the Jewish holiday Simchat Torah. The name literally means "rejoicing in the Torah" or "joy of the law." Typically celebrated in the fall, it marks the point in the year when synagogues finish reading the book of Deuteronomy and return to the beginning of the book of Genesis (Torah not only is "law" in an abstract sense but also signifies the first five books in the Jewish Bible or the Christian Old Testament). The five books of the Torah are read all the way through over the course of a year, so Simchat Torah marks the end of a cycle and beginning anew. Similar to how we mark the transition to a new year every December 31, Simchat Torah is a cause for celebration—it's a festival day marked by dancing in the synagogue with the scrolls of the Torah.

Dancing with the law! That blew my mind. If, as Christians insisted, the law was so oppressive—such a spiritual burden—why would anyone in their right mind *dance* with it? It reminded me of the famous quote often attributed to the early twentieth-century activist Emma Goldman: "If I can't dance, I don't want to be part of your revolution."

Christians often say that Jesus freed us from the law. But outside of the Pentecostal world, I don't know of any Christians inspired to actually dance as an expression of their joyful faith. The more I thought about this, the more I figured it was bigger than a debate between Christians and Jews. It's human nature to take something that is meant to set us free and turn it into a system of bureaucratic regulations. We see this at work within Christianity: it's a tradition built on the idea that Jesus sets us free, and yet too many voices within the tradition communicate the opposite message.

It occurred to me that the Christian idea of "Jesus frees us from the curse of the law" might actually (and more correctly) be restated as "Jesus frees us from how we sometimes misinterpret the law." It's not a *Jewish* problem that Jesus solves; it's a *human* problem—of getting caught up in a tendency to turn spiritual wisdom into statutes and obligations.

As I learned more about Jewish spirituality and how the Torah is meant to help us by introducing us to the very mind of God, I felt like I was discovering a new way of understanding Torah—as a love letter. This made me realize that my Christian upbringing taught me to see religious law (whether Jewish or Christian) more like a policy manual than as an expression of God's care. If we make the mistake of reading a love letter as a policy manual, we miss all the love and obsess over the rules. That strikes me as a recipe for spiritual fear rather than love. In learning to relate to the mind of God through love rather than fear, I could see that the more we fall in love with the mind of God, the more we long for it, desire it, want it soaking in our hearts and thoughts and imaginations. Which is a very good thing, for the "law of God" is not just encoded in the first five books of the Bible; it's also a gift given to each of us in our hearts.

According to the prophet Jeremiah, God makes a commitment to the people: "This is the covenant that I will make with the house of Israel after those days, says the Lord: I will put my law within them, and I will write it on their hearts; and I will be their God, and they shall be my people" (Jeremiah 31:33). Saint Paul, in his letter to the Romans, makes sure we know this gift of sacred law in our hearts refers to all people—Gentiles (non-Jews) also "show that what the law requires is written on their hearts, to which their own conscience also bears witness" (Romans 2:15).

The Hebrew word Jeremiah uses is directly related to Torah, and the Greek word that Paul uses, νόμος, *nomos*, shares the same root that we find in the English word *astronomy*—a word implying the natural order of things. Both Jeremiah and Paul are referring to law not in a political or controlling sense but in a this-is-the-nature-of-things sense, revealing a loving, life-giving divinity that flows throughout all nature.

It's no wonder that Christians (and others) are suspicious of the ways that laws can be used to control or oppress entire groups of people. We've seen too many examples of this abuse, such as the Jim Crow laws that made racism and the oppression of people of color in America "legal" (but no less wrong). Yet the "law in our hearts" is something entirely different from institutionalized legal codes. We need to open our minds and our hearts to such spiritually sourced "heart law"; this divine order held within us is a gift and that gift can calibrate us to the very mind of God. Far from just imposing a set of external precepts, the mind of God encoded in our hearts gives us a capacity to discern what is right, to oppose what is wrong, and to celebrate life.

Consider the experience of beauty. We all have cultural differences that can affect our taste in art, music, poetry, and so forth. But appreciating the splendor of a starry sky, the serene vastness of the ocean, or the majestic vista of a mountain range are pretty much universal human experiences. We might disagree on the details, but we all understand that there is such a thing as beauty, and we all want our lives to reflect it, however that beauty is found and appreciated. Also consider the nature of truth itself. It's a perennial challenge to sort out truth from lies or half-truths—that's what keeps mystery novelists, detectives, journalists, and TV scriptwriters in business.

As elusive as it might be, we keep looking for truth. We sort through the data or experience or phenomena to find what is consistent enough, stable enough, reliable enough, and verifiable enough to reach a consensus: this is true, these are the facts. It's part of human nature to believe not only that truth exists but also that it is the foundation of pretty much all knowledge, communication, law, justice—and our spiritual traditions as well.

We discover the law (read, "dancing joy") of God written in our hearts through these universals: goodness, beauty, truth. It's the mind of God in our hearts that makes it possible for us to translate languages, to find points of unity between religions, to negotiate treaties or business deals or cease-fires, to discern what is fair and good and true and beautiful—whether on a personal or a planetary level.

The divine law encoded in our hearts provides us with a basic resonance and affinity with not only what is truly real but also what is truly possible. Torah invites us to know the mind of God—and the *heart* of God as well. There's a reason why sacred writings suggest that the divine law is inscribed in our hearts rather than our minds. With the divine law written in our hearts giving us access to

> **We need to open our minds and our hearts to such spiritually sourced "heart law"; this divine order held within us is a gift.**

the very heart and mind of God, we may unite with that mystical divine mind through the power of our spiritual imagination—along with the silence that invites us to pray by listening to God's first language.

The law/mind of God given to us in our hearts speaks the language of the divine imagination—a language inscribed in our hearts. It's not a law that "tells us what to do—or else" but rather a law that opens us up to how God's universe operates, the universe encompassing all space and time as well as the infinity within our souls. The divine law helps us discern and create whatever is possible in this universe out of the serenity of silence and according to the artistry of our imagination.

We've looked at the Orthodox Christian understanding of prayer as a way for the mind to sink into the heart (and not the other way around). This suggests that the heart, spiritually speaking, is not only the source of the steady drumbeat of life but also the foundation for all of our human experience—even the mind's functions of consciousness and awareness, even including thought, feeling, and imagination. The heart is the foundation of what it means to be human.

I am not an expert on the science of the heart and mind. I approach this topic with the heart of a poet and the mind of a contemplative. But there are numerous researchers studying the heart-mind relationship from a scientific perspective, and authors like Paul Pearsall, Mimi Guarneri, and Doc Childre are working to make the science available to a mainstream audience.

As our knowledge of the biology of the heart deepens, it's become apparent that the human heart has its own intelligence, its own neurological network that makes it, after the brain, the body's second nerve center. We may not fully understand—at least scientifically speaking—how the brain-in-the-heart interacts with the "big brain," but consider the popular notion that the brain governs reason, logic, and thought, while the heart governs intuition, emotion, and inspiration. This understanding works in a symbolic or poetic sense as long as we see the heart-mind ecosystem as a creative partnership rather than a separation of powers.

It's a mistake to overstate the difference between heart and head. Different cultures have understood the relationship between mind and heart in different ways; for example, in Old Testament times, the heart was understood not just as the seat of emotion and intuition but rather as encompassing *all* of a person's interior life: vitality, intelligence, will, and even thought and imagination. In this way of understanding humanity, the brain (the "thought generator"—think of it as a bio-organic computer) exists to serve the heart, and not the other way around. Your heart, therefore, represents the fullness of who you are on the inside: conscious-ness and feeling, thought and intuition, reason and emotion, will and inspiration.

It is in this sense that the heart may be the natural home of our imagination and, for that matter, our intuition. As the law/mind of God is a gift we find in our hearts, so the heart functions as a fountain of dis-cernment as well.

Your heart repre-sents the fullness of who you are on the inside: consciousness and feeling, thought and intu-ition, reason and emotion, will and inspiration.

Cindy Lou Harrington, a musician as well as a special education teacher, wrote a song called "Language of the Heart" about her experience assisting children—among them my daughter—with special needs. The song tells the story of profoundly handicapped children who, although blind and incapable of speech, nevertheless have faces that light up when someone who cares for them walks into the room. As the song goes, "Somehow they know, deep in their heart, what has no ending, what has no start, it keeps on giving, when they're apart: the language of the heart." Is this a *way of knowing* that has less to do with sensory knowledge and mental calculation and more to do with an embodied intuition that we cannot measure or quantify?

Imagination, intuition, inspiration. These are the ways in which the heart makes sense of the world at large—how we do more than just weigh out all the data that flow through our eyes and ears to make decisions and gain understanding but actually bring a spirit of creativity and purpose to how we relate to ourselves, our loved ones, our neighbors near and far, and God.

"Imagination is your interior sense," the twentieth-century mystic Thomas Merton once told a group of his students at the Abbey of Gethsemani. "When you say imagination, you get into something pretty deep. . . . What normally people think of as imagination is simply fantasy . . . but imagination is not fantasy, imagination is creative. . . . The artist makes *you* an artist, whether you like it or not, or else you don't connect . . . what is the deepest part of yourself, your heart or your whole self. . . . It gets right into the depths of you."

Merton here is speaking of the imagination in a broadly mystical sense—far beyond the popular notion that the imagination is just the brain's capacity for make-believe. Imagination encompasses way more than just a movie that plays in our head; it is actually the capacity to generate possibilities and literally to create those possibilities—first in the theater within but then offering us the inspiration and energy to make what is envisioned within more than just an idea or a possibility but truly a reality. Think of Martin Luther King Jr.'s "I Have a Dream" speech, in which he spoke with an almost supernatural elegance of how he imagined a world beyond racism, where his "children will one day live in a nation where they will not be judged by the color of their skin but by the content of their character." I'm writing these words in the spring of 2020, when America is dealing with the horror of the murder of George Floyd, who was killed in a nauseating act of police brutality. It is a grim reminder that Dr. King's imagined/envisioned future still has not come to pass. But thank God for Dr. King's imagination and his vision—may it continue to guide us to share his imagination and do the work needed to dismantle racism in our country and beyond.

What does all this have to do with the gift of the divine law written in our hearts? When Dr. King was dreaming of a world where racism is obsolete, where freedom rings from the mountains and every town and village, where children play together regardless of their skin color, he was using his imagination to articulate a visionary future consistent with the law of God written in his heart. And in doing so, he discerned a possibility that did not exist before—at least not in the minds and hearts of many. And while we are discouraged by the fact that so little progress has been made in the ensuing half century, we can also recommit ourselves to his inspiring words, finding both meaning and our calling in how Martin Luther King Jr.'s dream remains more relevant—and urgent—than ever. He invited future generations to be inspired to create new ways to manifest the God-mind as a reality shared by all.

We need a Simchat Torah understanding of God's law written in our hearts—the law in our hearts that never condemns us but liberates us. It is a law that invites us to imagine all that is both possible and good and then to imagine ways to make it so. We need a creative, imaginative understanding that the key to discerning the very mind of God is encoded deep within us.

Still Augustine reminds us that we each possess a restless heart. With the mind and heart of God encoded deep within us already, why are we so restless? Could it be that our hearts cannot imagine anything higher or truer other than what we see? Could it be we are looking for love in all the wrong places, as the old Johnny

Lee song goes? What if we are restless not because we lack access to God but because God is so deeply integrated in our hearts that we feel restless every time we make choices that ignore or deny the truth of who we already are?

Could the pathway in our hearts be simply the road back to who we truly are? A path back to the authenticity of our truest and most beautiful self?

Trappist monk Elias Marechal, author of *Tears of an Innocent God*, describes the spiritual journey as a passage from the land of "unlikeness" to the land of "likeness"—to rediscovering the truth that we have already been created in the image and likeness of God. You cannot deface the image of God encoded in your DNA even if you set yourself to reject that image, choosing to live a life aligned with greed, violence, and hatred. The image of God remains in us.

We cannot erase the *image* of God, but most of us suffer from the *likeness* of God being hidden under our wounds and poor choices, choices that reject and thwart love. So we must walk the path of trials and challenges as we learn to release the claim that "unlikeness" has on us so that we might restore the likeness. This restoration only comes through the heart, through reimagining the truth that love is our natural birthright—that Love-with-a-capital-L is who we truly are.

Many of us suffer from the recognition of how unlike God we (and our lives) are. I'm reminded of the first of the Buddha's Four Noble Truths: life is shaped by suffering. I'm also reminded of Christ's beatitude "Blessed are those who mourn, for they will be comforted" (Matthew 5:4). The reality of knowing the mind of God, engraved in our hearts, is that even if we are not conscious of it, we will be stricken by how we are exiles in the land of unlikeness. We suffer because of the mistakes we have made and because of the mistakes of others. We suffer because of systemic problems—racism, sexism, or homophobia—that no one person is singularly responsible for, and yet all are plugged into evil systems that perpetrate harm, that benefit some while oppressing others. We suffer through the imperfections and randomness of nature, visiting upon some of us handicaps, birth defects, personality quirks, and talents (or the lack thereof) that can undermine natural happiness. We mourn, in short, because we look at the highway in our hearts and we see just how far it seems we have to go in order to restore that likeness within us—and within all creation.

We mourn for many other reasons as well—a loved one dies, a relationship ends, a financial or professional opportunity doesn't pan out. But perhaps the grief we feel at our losses, whether small or large, carries a sting because it always reminds us of the most fundamental loss we all live with: the loss caused by thinking we are separate from God.

It isn't so, but we think it is, so it feels real to us. Our imagination is creative, even when it creates something that harms us, like the illusion that God is far away. But when we allow it, the mind/law of God in our hearts can guide us to create more goodness, truth and beauty in our lives, and thus remind us of who we truly are.

Simchat Torah enables us to imagine an entirely new way of relating to God's law—as an invitation rather than a domination. An invitation to live, to dance, to imagine possibilities. God's law did not change when I learned a new way to think of it and to approach it. The only thing that changed was the story I told myself, in my own mind and heart, about God's law and what it meant for that law to be engraved in my heart. I suffered only when I forgot what the law within teaches.

There's an important principle here. Remember, the gift of silence marks God's presence in our hearts. By contrast, the gift of law marks God's presence not in terms of silence but in terms of language: words, principles, precepts, and decrees. Just as we may rest in silence to "be still and know God," so we may use words to express how we relate to God or describe God's law. Likewise, language shapes how we relate to ourselves, to one another, to the world at large.

In our exploration of the path of the heart, we have discovered two gifts that may seem paradoxical: the silence between every heartbeat and the law or mind of

God, which implies divine thoughts, divine language, divine words. How do these two integrate? Silence is simply silence; it has no language by definition. Spiritual practices such as contemplative prayer or mindfulness meditation often involve taking time to gently rest in silence, which means resting in a languageless place. By contrast, the gift of the law/mind of God points out that language, logic, and thought are just as important to spiritual growth as the silence of meditation or contemplation. In the imagination—that dimension of our hearts/minds where divine thought and divine generativity weave together—we can access the infinite possibilities of the mind of God and visualize how those possibilities might manifest in creative ways in our lives.

Every mystical or contemplative wisdom tradition seems to encompass a spirituality both of silence and also of sacred myths, stories, teachings, and rituals or liturgies. Every spiritual meditation practice—be it Christian, Buddhist, Hindu, or other—also includes, along with the practice of intentional/mindful silence, an emphasis on learning the language and stories of the tradition, which means we enter into the spiritual imagination of the tradition. These can be wildly divergent, and not all myths or sacred traditions are equal. Just within Christianity, for example, some traditions emphasize an image of God that is angry and wrathful, with a language of judgment around what "the law" means, beginning with the misunderstanding of Torah discussed earlier—seeing it as a rule book rather than a love letter. On the other hand, mystical or contemplative traditions within Christianity can be profoundly creative, optimistic, and joyful in their understanding of God as divine love and the spiritual life as an unfolding journey of responding ever more deeply to that love. I have found such creative expressions of Christianity among monks and nuns who have been the custodians of contemplative prayer practices, who make it part of their daily spirituality to chant the Psalms, to engage in liturgical prayer, and to read the sacred Scriptures.

Even the most austerely silent monastery still makes room for learning the wisdom teachings, engaging in the liturgies, and cultivating creative understandings of who God is and what it means to be a spiritual person. Such "content-rich" practices are important within a mystical or contemplative tradition because they help the practitioner cultivate his or her spiritual imagination in conjunction with contemplative disciplines that lead them ever more deeply into the divine silence that is "God's first language."

Cultivating the spiritual imagination can be an important way in which the heart's capacity for discernment is brought to our consciousness.

As we get to know the gifts of the heart, we find that meditation and contemplation are spiritual practices that entrain us to the silence between every heartbeat.

Imaginal practices (for example, imaginative prayer, or *lectio divina*) offer a complementary invitation: they call us to engage with language (or images or symbols) that can help us find the law of God encoded in our hearts. And having found the mind of God encoded there, we may celebrate the possibilities that the divine presence makes continually available in our lives—emerging from our hearts.

Cultivating the spiritual imagination can be an important way in which the heart's capacity for discernment is brought to our consciousness, which comes through words even as it may be informed by silence. Between every heartbeat is silence. Between every thought is silence. Between every moment of imaginal seeing, the vast limitlessness of silence remains within us. Discernment, shaped by the silent intuition of the heart as well as the received wisdom of our spiritual ancestors and foremothers/forefathers, can help guide our imaginations into a more fully loving and creative response to the silent whisper of the Spirit within us.

Learning to cultivate the creative imagination takes practice, as does learning to calibrate our lives to the law in our hearts that represents the heart/mind of God. It requires discernment as we remember that the imagination and pure silence are two different (if complementary) experiences of the heart/mind of God. The imagination is like the heartbeat: it's muscular, powerful, and sustains life. Contemplation and meditation are like the moments of rest between each heartbeat: they open us up to the spaciousness of eternity and to the presence of God, which transcends all language. To walk along the highway of the heart, we need both.

Heart Practice:
Lectio Divina

Lectio divina (Latin for "divine reading" or "sacred reading") has become a popular spiritual practice for Christians interested in a contemplative approach to reading the Bible. While its roots involve a sacred encounter with biblical writings, lectio divina can be applied to other wisdom writings not only within Christianity but from other mystical or contemplative traditions as well.

If you're not familiar with it, the process is very simple: unlike reading a book to gather information or to master an idea, with lectio divina, the emphasis is on reading slowly and prayerfully, entering the words you read in an imaginal way, keeping in mind that this is an encounter between you and the God who meets us in the words of the sacred text. Think of lectio divina as an immersion into the imaginative mystery. This practice typically involves choosing a short passage and reading it slowly—perhaps rereading it several times or simply stopping as soon as a word or a phrase seems to jump out at you with a meaning or insight especially for you. Once you read the text and find or choose the word/phrase, then the next step is to meditate thoughtfully on the word(s), mulling over them and considering what insights or meaning might emerge for you. When the meditation seems fulfilled, the process moves to praying about the insights you receive, no matter how small or insignificant they may be. Finally, after the prayer feels complete, you finish the process by simply resting in silence, allowing God to be lovingly present to you.

Consider how this exercise builds on and integrates the first two practices we explored. First we paid attention to our hearts' longings, then we entered into the imaginal space within our hearts. Now we braid together prayerful silence and the imagination with the words of our (or any) sacred tradition. By doing so, these words may slowly form us into the likeness of God (that is already hidden deep in our hearts). It's a slow process, like water dripping on a stone slowly carves a groove. That's okay; we have all of eternity for the Spirit to form and reform the divine likeness within us. It's never too late to begin a spiritual practice like lectio divina, and whenever we begin, the spiritual blessings begin to manifest in our lives as we seek to become more intimate with the wisdom writings that call to us. When we allow the words from sacred Scripture or other mystical texts to ignite our imagination and illuminate our hearts' longings, we can enter into that place where creativity emerges—a place where we recognize the mind of God within our hearts and allow that wisdom encoded deep within us to shape our lives to both receive and share wisdom and blessings.

4

RENEWAL

Can our hearts make mistakes? I know I like to think that "listening to my heart" is a fail-safe way to align myself with my highest spiritual good. But discernment implies that sometimes we have to sort out conflicting ideas and perspectives that don't always add up to what's best. Sometimes even our hearts may make mistakes, which is something I've learned from my own life.

I was not an athletic child, and by the time I got to middle school and high school, most of my attention was focused on academics. Physical education was a requirement that had to be endured, not an hour I enjoyed. By the time I graduated from college, I thought I would never darken the door of a gymnasium again. For years, I kept reasonably healthy through social or outdoor activities, such as hiking or dancing. It wasn't until I got into my fifties that doctors began pointing out to me that the pounds I had been slowly adding on over the years were not going to magically disappear. Then my stepdaughter passed away after a long illness, and during the anguished, grieving eighteen months following her death, I gained twenty-five pounds.

One day I went to a local fitness center and got a two-week free pass; one conversation with a savvy salesperson later, not only had I joined, but I signed up for a year's worth of weekly appointments with a personal trainer.

It wasn't easy adopting an entirely new habit. I told my trainer, a muscle-ripped young fellow named Derek just out of the navy (whose arms were about as big as my legs), that I literally had not lifted weights since I was in graduate school. He smiled and praised me for being there now, and then we got to work.

As I watched the pounds melt off my abdomen—and my self-confidence increase—I began to wonder why I hadn't joined a fitness center years before. But I knew why.

As a youth, I felt ashamed in the locker room because I was so unathletic. Without realizing it, as an adult, I had turned that childhood shame into a self-deceiving pride, thinking I didn't need a gymnasium to stay healthy—until, of course, I did.

Learning to face down that demon of shame taught me an important lesson. When I finally chose to do something good for myself, I discovered the profound difference between toxic shame and authentic humility.

Humility allowed me to recognize I would never keep up with younger people at the gym—and that was okay. This wasn't about impressing anybody; I just wanted to (finally) take care of myself in my own humble way.

I spent three decades thinking the antidote to shame was avoidance, when in fact, a down-to-earth spirit of humility was all that I needed. In other words, for thirty years, I deceived myself about a very simple but important matter: taking good care of myself.

As we continue to travel the pathway of the heart, some words from the prophet Jeremiah deserve careful attention: "The heart is devious above all else; it is perverse—who can understand it?" (Jeremiah 17:9).

One day, after I posted something positive about the gifts of the heart on social media, someone responded by quoting this verse from Jeremiah and adding something along the lines of "You can't trust your heart at all."

When I read the person's dismissive comment, as if this one cautionary verse from Jeremiah negated every positive statement ever made about the heart in the Bible and all other wisdom literature of the ages, I felt a familiar feeling: a sense of religious shame.

It's something I learned as a child. I attended a conservative church where I was taught that the most important fact about the human condition was "We are all terrible sinners." If you were guilty of just one minor sin, in the eyes of God you were as depraved as a mass murderer.

Later on while studying church history, I learned that the Protestant reformer John Calvin even came up with a way to describe this pessimistic view of humanity: the doctrine of total depravity. Deriving from Augustine's idea of original sin, total depravity considers the human condition as utterly broken and therefore inherently corrupt; we are only capable of any good intention or action because of God's grace and activity in our lives.

If that's the way you see the world, then calling the heart devious, deceitful, tortuous, perverse, or beyond remedy or cure makes sense—in a twisted kind of way.

But how does that line up with all the gifts and graces in our hearts? The pilgrim's pathway, contemplative silence, the law (mind) of God, and so many other gifts that we have yet to consider? Again and again, the Jewish and Christian Scriptures sing the heart's praises. Proverbs, for example, proclaims, "Keep your heart with all vigilance, for from it flow the springs of life" (Proverbs 4:23). "Flowing springs of life" certainly doesn't have the same negative vibe as "devious above all else." Clearly, we need a nuanced understanding to make sense of how the heart may be imperfect but remains a fountain of blessings within us.

Is every human heart devious and deceitful? Sometimes they can be. We all are capable of lying to ourselves, of fooling ourselves, of rationalizing away truths we do not want to face. This is why folks in the recovery movement keep saying, "Denial is not a river." This is true of the college student who refuses to admit he has a drinking problem, the overzealous entrepreneur who cannot acknowledge that her business is failing, and the elderly person who insists he is still capable of living alone even after repeated falls or incidents that point to cognitive impairment.

We all are susceptible to self-deception. While sometimes this might be just a matter of false swagger—something that deep down you know is not true—it seems that there are times when we trick ourselves so thoroughly that we act with what we think is integrity, and only others (or ourselves at a later date) can see the problem.

What the prophet Jeremiah makes clear is that everyone is susceptible to self-deception. Even the most self-aware, psychologically mature, spiritually healthy person is still capable on some level of fooling themselves, especially about something that they might consciously view in a disapproving way. I write this knowing this applies to me as much as to anyone. Everyone can be a trickster sometimes, even if the only person we delude is ourselves.

What do we do, knowing our capacity for self-deception resides in the same heart from which springs of life flow? Just being suspicious isn't the answer; to adopt an attitude of mistrust toward everything that emerges from deep within would also mean mistrusting the springs of life—and all the inner gifts we have been given.

The law of God in our hearts gives us the ability to discern between what tends to nurture life and what may diminish it. We need to apply that discernment to the heart itself—to sort out what tends to deceive from what tends to foster vibrant life. We have to be discerning about everything—even our own hearts.

Discernment is not the same thing as suspicion, nor is it a type of paranoia. It's simply a matter of humbly noticing that sometimes, what seems like a great idea or a self-evident truth might not fly when you present it to your family and friends, or the world at large, or ultimately, with careful consideration, even to yourself.

Jeremiah's words are a warning, but they aren't the last word. They don't even offer a way forward to affirm the good wisdom of the heart. If we see the heart as basically devious, we'll never be able to trust it (or ourselves). Such mistrust short-circuits our hope and our imagination and renders us incapable of doing the good things that flow like a spring from our hearts, which include not only reaching our full potential as human beings but also working for justice and peace and anything else which is truly good.

When we keep them in the proper perspective, Jeremiah's words offer wise counsel. It's prudent to remember that the heart is not infallible; it can make mistakes. Let your imagination soar and meet it with discernment. Trust your heart, but don't give it a blank check. On occasion it stumbles. Sometimes it gets sick and needs care, or healing, or even a transplant.

Another Old Testament prophet, Ezekiel, offers a different perspective to Jeremiah's dour assessment. At a time when Ezekiel saw the people of Israel being unfaithful to God, he prophesied that God wanted to heal the relationship. Speaking in the voice of God, Ezekiel proclaimed, "I will sprinkle clean water upon you, and you shall be clean from all your uncleannesses, and from all your idols I will cleanse you. A new heart I will give you, and a new spirit I will put within you; and I will remove from your body the heart of stone and give you a heart of flesh. I will put my spirit within you, and make you follow my statutes and be careful to observe my ordinances" (Ezekiel 36:25–27).

> **Let your imagination soar and meet it with discernment. Trust your heart, but don't give it a blank check.**

Here is the next gift given to us in our hearts: the gift of renewal. Sometimes, it is true, a heart can deceive; such a heart is a heart of stone. When our hearts turn to stone, we are promised the gift of a new heart, a new spirit—a heart of living flesh from which living waters flow.

This gift anticipates one of the greatest promises in Scripture: the promise of the Spirit, "poured into our hearts through the Holy Spirit that has been given to us" (Romans 5:5). And it is Ezekiel who links the gift of the Spirit to an observance of the divine law and the gift of a *new* heart—a heart of flesh, not of stone.

When we remember that the divine law (the mind of God) is not some religious ploy to subject us to a rigid set of rules or legal constraints, we can see this in a luminous way. The statutes and ordinances Ezekiel mentions point us back to the Torah—the very mind/ heart/imagination of God. We are given the Spirit of God in our hearts in order to be renewed and restored to the divine likeness.

God eagerly seeks to replace our stony hearts with hearts of flesh. While on a purely physical level, this evokes the idea of a transplant, on a spiritual or poetic level, we can see this as a "transplant" from the heart that deceives to the heart that receives the divine spirit humbly, authentically, and joyfully.

The gift of a renewed heart is, in essence, the gift of new life. We are all radiant creatures of divine love, fashioned of stardust and almost limitlessly creative. Yes, we make mistakes and sometimes we do foolish or harmful things. But the gift of a renewed heart reminds us that we are so much more than our foibles, our errors, or our sins. We are luminous beings, to borrow a line from Yoda. Our hearts are brimming with gifts of life and love that guide us on a pathway that leads us to joy.

But what if someone's stony heart *doesn't* get renewed? We all meet people who just seem to be calibrated toward meanness, or abuse, or self-centeredness, or bitterness, or any of a host of qualities that seem to sap life rather than nourish it. Sometimes these life-leaching qualities accompany a person all the way to physical death. What then?

To speak honestly about our hearts' capacities to turn to stone, we also have to acknowledge this truth: life leads to death. Even a renewed heart will someday die. How does death fit into the gifts of the heart? Certainly, every life has a measure of spiritual or symbolic "deaths." I always imagine that the lessons of our spiritual deaths/endings help us prepare spiritually for the ultimate transition that comes when we physically die, when our hearts stop beating.

Between birth and death are numerous stages and ages and cycles of life. The baby becomes the toddler, who becomes the child, who becomes the adolescent, and so forth. Seasons of our lives "die" when new seasons begin: graduation, marriage, career change, children, health crises, retirement . . . death, even if symbolic, is a part of every life.

More than once in my professional career, I remained working at jobs longer than was good for me, vocationally or emotionally. At least once I remained in a romantic relationship for too long. We can look back and too easily see the mistakes we made in the past when we thought we were keeping something alive that wasn't ready to die, but in fact, we merely feared its death (even just the death of a job or romance). This is yet another example of how our hearts can deceive us, driving our fearful choices rather than welcoming new life into us. I recall moments when I moved from keeping situations like those on life support to finally letting them go. When at last I surrendered my resistance and accepted the "death," the release was a blessing all around.

Death, even in a spiritual or psychological sense, is never easy, and it seems to be hardwired in us to fight it or flee from it. But we have to let the stony heart die to receive the gift of renewal that will come with our new heart of flesh. God wants to restore us, to heal us, to prepare us for the transitions and transformations that life brings our way.

I suppose this explains why I feel so confident about life after death even though I have no idea what form that ultimately will take. It just seems to be so natural that because life is filled with seasons of birth, growth, maturity, decline, and death only to be followed by new birth in some form, even the awe-inspiring finality of physical death can only be a prelude to a beatific renaissance.

God wants to give us renewed hearts thrumming with life. Sometimes our old hearts can be saved before they get too stony, but there will always be those times when our hearts, spiritually speaking, will calcify and require a heart transplant, which can only happen when we release our existential fear in order to receive the new heart being offered to us. A "spiritual heart transplant" has plenty of unknowns. When God gives us our new hearts of flesh, how will things be different? What will be required of us? Will our new hearts steer us away from old relationships only to find new ones to cherish? Will we have to reorient our lives to the demands of these new hearts, calibrated as they are to the mind and heart of God?

These are real questions, and the unknowing can seem daunting. But we can trust the promise of a new heart, just as we trust a new dawn each morning or a new spring each year. A new heart truly represents new life. If we turn it down, we simply diminish ourselves. But when we say yes, we embrace a novel world of new possibilities.

I've heard monks say that the monastic life can be summed up like this: "I fall down, I get up; I fall down, I get up." Richard Rohr wrote a book called *Falling Upward*, which suggests that such descending can be a learning and a renewal. Falling down and rising again is a powerful archetypal image of spirituality. The Bible—or at least the way it's been interpreted for many centuries now—is built on this idea: Adam fell, and Jesus offered a way to get humanity back on its feet again. Likewise, the Buddha "fell" when he forswore the life of a prince to become a spiritual seeker, only to make a string of mistakes—like abandoning his wife and child or punishing his body with extreme disciplines—but then he "got up" again with his enlightenment under the Bodhi tree. And Plotinus, the great pagan Greek mystic, saw the entire structure of the cosmos in terms of "falling" from unity with the One, only to "return" through meditation, wisdom, and spiritual discipline. When I neglected caring for my body and gained weight from eating too much comfort food, I fell. And then, between the grace of God and acknowledging that I needed help, I got back up by joining the gym and humbly following the instructions of my personal trainer. Granted, that's hardly at the level of awakening beneath a Bodhi tree, but it's an example of what even a small "getting up" can mean.

When the heart deceives us, we fall. Then something deeper in our hearts calls us back to who we truly are, and we get back up. When our hearts turn to stone, that deeper something offers us renewal with a new heart of flesh. And the cycle repeats itself in different ways or different forms. That doesn't make the heart unreliable; it just helps us remember how important it is to listen to our hearts with discernment and a commitment to truth, integrity, and authenticity.

When we don't listen deeply enough, when we allow our hearts to deceive us, we can cause harm not only to ourselves but to others. For example, as a white man, I am conscious of how my heart can accept the deceit of white supremacy, which means I participate in a system that causes grave harm to others. Howard Thurman, the African American mystic and Baptist preacher who mentored Martin Luther King Jr., tells a horrific story of ongoing, everyday racism he faced during the Jim Crow era. He recounts traveling on a train from Chicago to Memphis; the train was not segregated, but apparently some passengers thought it ought to be. Thurman wrote, "I found a seat across from an elderly lady, who took immediate cognizance of my presence. When the conductor came along for the tickets, she said to him, pointing in my direction, 'What is *that* doing in this car?' The conductor answered, with a touch of creative humor, '*That* has a ticket.'"

Unfortunately, the woman could not leave matters alone. Thurman described her going on to talk to all the other white passengers in the coach at length to express her dismay that a Black man was sitting among them. Thurman—the renowned minister, author, and spiritual leader—concludes his record of the event, writing, "I was able to see the atmosphere in the entire car shift from common indifference to active recognition of and, to some extent, positive resentment of my presence; an ill will spreading its virus by contagion."

No mere relic of the past, Thurman's encounter with such explicit prejudice is something we still witness—and frankly, contribute to—daily. Racism and white privilege poison our society in uncountable ways: Black communities and communities of color experience microaggressions, police brutality, economic and social barriers, biases in our justice system and every other system and institution, bringing harm, diminishing communities, and creating risks that privileged white persons never encounter. The Black Lives Matter movement has sought to protect Black communities and educate the general public about how law enforcement systems are inherently racist—even as many white persons refuse to look at the plain evidence of how discrimination continues to undermine the lives and well-being of so many people.

Such racism, privilege, and complacency simply represent more evidence of Jeremiah's deceitful heart—hearts in need of the gift of renewal. And hearts that require discernment to truly see the truth of the harm we perpetrate.

The harm we've done to others—even subconsciously or as a result of our privilege—is our own falling down. And we are called to get back up by making real changes in our lives that contribute to dismantling systems of privilege and oppression rather than ignoring or tolerating them. We always have the possibility of getting back up. The Spirit is always ready to remove the deceit in our hearts when we are willing to let it go.

When Jesus was crucified, it looked like a tragedy. A charismatic young rabbi had fallen afoul of the authorities, and they killed him for it. It marked the end of something that could have been beautiful. But it wasn't the end.

Gandhi was killed, but his philosophy of peace inspired Howard Thurman and Martin Luther King Jr. to launch the civil rights movement. George Floyd was murdered by a cop, and a national uprising changed the stony hearts of many to flesh, and they joined the struggle for racial justice. And Jesus's death led to the greatest plot twist in history: the resurrection, setting into motion the chain of events that led to Pentecost and the birth of the Christian wisdom tradition.

> The harm we've done to others—even subconsciously or as a result of our privilege—is our own falling down. And we are called to get back up by making real changes in our lives that contribute to dismantling systems of privilege and oppression.

"Blessed are the persecuted," one of the most confusing beatitudes begins. Is this a kind of romanticizing of the victim? No one rejoices in the "goodness" of persecution. What was Jesus trying to say? Is it that those who suffer persecution or oppression in service of the truth have solace in knowing that God is with them, suffers with them? Is such solace the promised blessing, even if such knowledge does nothing to stop the injustice? On a more dynamic level, does this blessing mean that those who have been persecuted and oppressed can lead us, collectively, into justice and new life? The American civil rights movement could have only come about because of the vision and the leadership of African American heroes like Martin Luther King Jr., Howard Thurman, Bayard Rustin, and Rosa Parks. The struggle for the rights of LGBTQ persons required the leadership of people like Barbara Gittings, Harvey Milk, Audre Lorde, and Sarah McBride.

Perhaps the persecuted are blessed because they lead the way to a more just and fair and peaceful world—for all of us. They are the midwives of our collective renewed hearts.

"Blessed are the persecuted" is a beatitude in two parts. Jesus said, "Blessed are those who are persecuted for righteousness' sake," but then he gets personal: "Blessed are you when people revile you and persecute you and utter all kinds of evil against you falsely on my account" (Matthew 5:10–11). Jesus knew what he was doing by emphasizing righteousness in a general sense before mentioning those who suffer for their loyalty to him. Religious identity is not always the most reliable marker of spiritual health or well-being. This beatitude challenges us to acknowledge the harm caused by persecution and oppression. When people are victimized because of their sexuality or gender identity or skin color or cultural difference, they can be blessed because they bear witness to the brokenness in our world, highlighting our collective need for renewed hearts. They become fellow sufferers of Jesus and hold the light of blessing for others.

The Buddhist writer Sylvia Boorstein once observed, "Compassion is the natural response of the heart unclouded by the specious view that we are separate from one another." Thinking we are separate from one another is just another way we can deceive ourselves. Remembering that we are all interconnected—all one in our common humanity—and the good action it inspires is yet another sign of the gift of a renewed heart.

This dynamic of stony hearts renewed, of falling down and rising again, reminds me of temperance— one of the fruits of the Spirit. Temperance (also translated into English as "self-control" or "self-restraint") comes from a Greek word that means "having power over oneself." It's the capacity to set healthy boundaries over our own behavior. It's the raw material of discipline and sustained healthy choices. It's not wasting time shaming ourselves when we make mistakes or fall off the wagon or don't bother to go to the gym. Temperance is the power to do the right thing as soon as we realize there's a wrong that needs to be made right. When that wrong involves harming others, our "getting up" consists of the concrete steps we take to correct the situation. Temperance is more interested in getting back on the wagon or doing what needs to be done than in squandering energy revisiting shame, which can result in spiritual paralysis or even further harm.

Temperance, like discernment, helps us sort out what deceives us from what gives us life. Both temperance and discernment point to hope—hope even for when we make mistakes or cause harm. "Our help is in the name of the Lord, who made heaven and earth," one psalmist writes (Psalm 124:8). The One who gave us our hearts to begin with, who gives us in our hearts gifts of silence and discernment and a path to follow, who replaces the stoniness of a deceitful heart with the renewed life of a fleshly heart, and who empowers us with the ability to make things right—that is the One in whom we should place our ultimate trust. By trusting God, we trust that we shall receive the gifts we need to choose wisely, and choose wisely again, all the days of our lives.

Heart Practice:
Fasting

For Jesus and Benedict and many mystics through the ages, fasting was a normal part of spiritual practice. It goes against the grain of our contemporary culture, where the emphasis on human fulfillment and personal growth tends to cast everything—even spirituality—in terms of what feels good, what offers immediate results, and what seems psychologically sensible. But fasting provides a new perspective for spiritual growth. Intentionally refraining from food and drink makes sense when it calls attention to something beyond itself. We can fast in many ways beyond abstaining from food; for example, a practice that has become increasingly popular in our time is a "technology fast" or "social media fast." Making a conscious decision to disengage from social media can call attention to our seemingly incessant need for online stimulation—and why we turn to it in order to "fill" ourselves. Meanwhile, even the traditional type of fasting can serve a noble cause, such as when a hunger strike is employed to highlight an injustice.

Fasting is commended in many spiritual traditions. Muslims fast during the month of Ramadan. Many Orthodox and Catholic Christians fast or abstain from certain foods during Lent. Such disciplines may have fallen out of favor because they seem to imply a spirituality that is hostile to the body—seeing the body as somehow inferior to the spirit and therefore needing to be punished or chastised. But this is a misunderstanding of both the original intent and the spiritual benefit of fasting and other ascetical practices.

Asceticism is an intimidating word, but it merely means "training" or "exercise"; it carries the same sense of spiritual empowerment as does temperance. The Cistercian monk André Louf wrote, "All Christian ascetic effort must bring about a sort of breaking of the heart; it must bring one to the point of nothingness of which we have spoken to make place for the power and the grace of Jesus." This is not hostility to our bodies but an invitation for an embodied participation in the falling and getting back up of the Spirit, of whose divine nature we all partake. We break our stony hearts to open ourselves for the grace of a renewed heart. When we fast, we do not shame ourselves because we like to eat; rather, we are creating the space to touch physical hunger as a way of remembering our more foundational spiritual hunger. Or perhaps instead of breaking the heart, fasting leads to a softening of the stony heart in order to discern and make room for the heart of renewed life, which is continually given to us by the Spirit who loves us.

Be gentle when you first explore the spirituality of fasting. Perhaps once a month, skip a meal, and a few times each year, skip meals for an entire day. Donate the money you would have spent on food to the poor. When fasting, if possible, withdraw into solitude for prayer and meditation, paying attention to your body to acknowledge the hunger that arises or listening to your heart as it quiets enough to hear what surfaces. When you break your fast, consider how the pleasure of the food you are eating represents the sacred pleasure of a heart fully open to the love of God.

If you would like to try a technology fast, consider choosing one day a week when anything in your life that has a screen—television, computer, cell phone, other portable devices—is turned off for twenty-four hours. Notice the "hunger" that emerges (or even the anxiety at merely thinking about it). Consider this as an opportunity for discernment, listening with humility as your media hunger highlights something your heart may lack or a need you might notice for renewal and new life. Remember, this process is meant to foster not shame but rather a humble acknowledgment of our imperfections (we fall down) and the consequent need for the grace that renews (we get up, and get up again).

5

WISDOM

My stepdaughter, Rhiannon, born with polycystic kidney disease, suffered a debilitating stroke at age three, which left her confined to a wheelchair and with limited mobility skills for the rest of her life.

Navigating life from a wheelchair created a number of challenges for Rhiannon and for my wife, Fran, and me. She lacked the ability to get in and out of her chair without help—to get herself out of bed or use the toilet without assistance.

Life with Rhiannon always moved at a very slow pace.

If we decided to drive up to Virginia to visit my parents for the holidays, we would travel in our van, which was equipped with a hydraulic lift for getting Rhiannon in and out of the vehicle. After we hooked her wheelchair to the van floor with retractable straps, keeping the chair safely in place, we would pack in our luggage, Christmas presents, and other essential items, such as her roll-in shower chair / commode, and off we would go on our journey. Naturally, on any long journey, eventually you have to stop to use the restroom. Traveling with Rhiannon, even something that simple became a complex process. We would stop, open the van, pull all our luggage out, and get Rhiannon out. Then usually Fran would accompany her into the restroom and assist her as needed, while I would stay with the van and our luggage, watching over it until the time came for Rhiannon to get back into the vehicle.

What for others would be a ten-minute stop could take us half an hour or more. My point in recounting this is not to complain—on the contrary. It is to appreciate how caring for Rhiannon meant learning to move slowly, at a pace that allowed us to meet the challenges associated with her handicap and the special needs connected to her care.

Rhiannon, by the necessities of her disability, taught me two very precious things: she taught me patience, and she taught me that life can move at a very slow pace without ever sacrificing beauty or love.

Spiritually speaking, patience can mean the capacity to rest in the silence between each heartbeat. It implies a quality of slowness—an ability to be slow to anger, to frustration, to conflict. Even when the heart is speeding up because the flight-or-fight response has been activated in our bodies, patience speaks an embodied language we often forget when a perceived threat emerges. The flight-or-fight impulse, which helped our ancestors stay alive for countless generations, may not always be useful in today's world, where the "threat" may simply be the normal flow of human conflict or the challenges of adjusting to the necessary constraints of life in the urban jungle.

If I had lashed out (or withdrew) every time I had been frustrated with how Rhiannon's handicap slowed us down, I would have been a terrible father and husband, and my marriage would not have lasted very long.

Patience, as an embodied alternative to the fight-or-flight impulse, represents an evolution of the body and mind—and heart. Any species evolves, over many generations, to adapt to changing circumstances in its environment. The tendency to attack or retreat is hardwired in us. For example, watch children on a playground. It doesn't take long for a scuffle to erupt when two or more of them fall into a conflict, while at the periphery, you're likely to find one or more kids who felt safer by leaving the chaotic scene or waiting it out on the sidelines, uninterested in getting involved. The capacity to respond to challenging or threatening situations with patience is a choice nurtured over time. Ironically, this fruit of the Spirit must be cultivated slowly—it takes patience to become patient.

Some wise guy once quipped, "God, I want patience, and I want it *now*!" We laugh at the absurdity of this because we understand that patience needs to emerge slowly over time. A child who is impulsive and can barely wait for Christmas to arrive strikes us as amusing (unless our own patience is being tried). But if a thirty-year-old displays a similar inability to wait, we wonder what's wrong with them. As for elders, we admire when they display calm patience, especially in the face of pain or suffering; such forbearance is evidence of the wisdom associated with age.

If there were a taxonomy of virtues, wisdom and patience would be grouped together. Like patience, wisdom is a quality, a virtue, which typically emerges over time: we think of *wise* and *old* going together, but not *wise* and *young*. A young person might be brash, clever, a prodigy, or just plain smart—but wisdom we associate with maturity.

Be that as it may, wisdom is the next gift promised to us in our hearts.

The book of Proverbs explains how wisdom is given to us in our hearts: "For the Lord gives wisdom . . . for wisdom will come into your heart, and knowledge will be pleasant to your soul" (Proverbs 2:6, 10). Like all the other blessings in our hearts, wisdom is simply given; such gifts are available to us merely by virtue of being human. We don't have to earn them, or prove ourselves worthy of them, or otherwise angle for a reward. Gifts are simply given to be received. No strings attached.

But another line from the psalms offers us an additional and perhaps more nuanced perspective on the gift of wisdom: "Teach us to count our days that we may gain a wise heart" (Psalm 90:12). This suggests that a gift given but never received or used is a gift wasted. You can have the most remarkable library in the world, but without making the effort to read the great works of literature and philosophy in your possession, it will profit you little. The gift of wisdom in our hearts

> If there were a taxonomy of virtues, wisdom and patience would be grouped together.

operates much the same way. Freely given, wisdom must be "gained"—which is to say, accepted. Will we? Will we learn to use it? Will we apply it to each counted day of our lives? Meanwhile, that the psalmist linked wisdom with "counting our days" makes me think of patience again: wisdom is a gift that may be given to us in our hearts, but we "gain" it by patiently counting our days—discovering the insight and perspective that only a life patiently and fully lived may yield.

When you slow down enough to listen to the silence between your heartbeats, you discover the freedom to choose something other than fight or flight, and you recognize the capacity within yourself to make such a choice with intention and commitment. That is how patience unlocks the gift of wisdom in the heart.

"Teach us to count our days" is a poetic way of saying that we gain real wisdom slowly. Wisdom is given to us in our hearts, but that doesn't mean we have *wise* hearts. At least, not at first.

Learn to count your days; learn to be patient. To gain wisdom takes time.

Wisdom and patience are spiritually bonded. In developing one, you foster the other, and vice versa. Just like you learn to work out certain groups of muscles in tandem, it makes sense that certain spiritual gifts naturally develop together. Generosity and trust grow together. So do patience and wisdom. So do joy and love.

Sharing sinews, they are still different. Wisdom means more than just patience. Wisdom emerges out of the union of learning and love. It's widened by patience. A wise capacity to understand and to recognize is the fruit of mature knowledge. But knowledge without love can be cold and impersonal, logical like Mr. Spock but incapable of appreciating the nuances of kinship and relationship and how they impact our lives and our legacies. Wisdom requires love as much as it requires knowledge, where the ability to understand and discern must be tempered with a capacity for compassion and caring.

The blessings of patience and wisdom emerge after we have been on the spiritual path for some time. These are not typically the graces we find at the beginning of the journey; they build on the gifts that have come before them even while they prepare us for the challenges and graces yet to come.

The spiritual path leads us on a journey pulsating with the rhythm of life. The heart pumps, then it rests. Beat, then silence. This is so basic to our biology that it barely needs comment. Every day is a cadence of sunlight and night, each year a reprise of the four seasons. In church settings, so much of the ritual or liturgical imagination takes us on a journey that is both rhythmical and cyclical, from Advent to Christmas, from Epiphany to Ash Wednesday, from Holy Week and Easter to Pentecost before returning to Advent once again. So much of the work we do is likewise cyclical—managing a farm or a factory follows a natural repetition, a predictable recurrence of basic tasks.

> **Wisdom helps us navigate the cycles of life and to be patient with their ordinary ups and downs.**

Even our falling and rising (I fall down, and I get back up) has its own rhythm. Wisdom is a gift that makes it possible to discern the presence of God—of divine love in both descending and ascending.

Wisdom helps us navigate the cycles of life and to be patient with their ordinary ups and downs. When we abandon childhood to enter adolescence, that earlier season of our lives is gone forever. The lessons we learn and the skills we gain follow a linear progression. It is this gradual dynamic of growth that enables us to "gain" our wise hearts. The path in our hearts cycles back around to familiar cadences again and again, but each cycle also takes us forward a step at a time. As we fall down and get back up again and again, we learn in our humble way to have a sense of humor about it all—since, after all, making mistakes is an unavoidable part of life. Then when something happens on our journey to teach us or inspire us or otherwise move us forward along the one-way path, we are transformed in a way that can never be undone.

How do these related virtues of patience and wisdom inform the problem we first considered in chapter 1, the restlessness in our hearts? Our hearts are often restless because even when we believe God is present in all things, we often do not feel it or sense it (we remain lost in the cloud of unknowing). Patience and wisdom are important nutrients for the spiritual life that can help us learn to recognize the divine presence in our hearts and in our lives even when it seems hidden from us.

The concept of apotheosis might shed some light on this. *Apotheosis* is a Greek word that means "revealing the divinity within" (think of the Greek word for "revelation," *apocalypse*, and you can get a sense of this). Unfortunately, it's a word that is frequently used with a more watered-down meaning. Often apotheosis is used in English as meaning "climax" or "high point." Critics will remark that the Ninth Symphony was Beethoven's apotheosis when what they mean is merely that it was his masterpiece, his greatest composition—not that it revealed his inner divinity. Spiritually speaking, our apotheosis refers to that transforming moment when we recognize who we really are: we sense that God loves us unconditionally, that God created us in the divine image and likeness, and that God truly is present in all things, even in our flesh and blood. By comprehending this bit of mystical insight, we may even find the divine presence within us.

Even the presence of God seems to have a cyclical quality in our hearts and minds. Or maybe what's cyclical is the rhythm of how we notice the divine presence but then "forget it" until we notice again. But we can discern a linear quality to this presence as well: There's a moment in our lives, whether we are nine or nineteen or ninety-two, when we first begin to suspect there's something divine within. We are changed. We think, *God and I are not-two.* Initially we may have no idea what this really means, but we have a clear sense that we've met something we need to explore. God loves us so much that God has filled our hearts with so many gifts—including the gift of wisdom, even though it may only manifest once we've learned to "count the days." Wisdom emerges as we come to understand that all love, all knowledge, all patience, and indeed, all virtue come from one source. When I can see that there are blessings in my heart, I can recognize my connection to that source of blessing and discover that I am part of that source. In the words of the second letter of Peter, we are "participants of the divine nature" (2 Peter 1:4). We recognize that this is a process, yet with each glimmer of recognition, we receive hints of our own apotheosis—our own capacity to recognize the divine within, that divine nature in which we partake.

What steps must we take to gain the gift of wisdom, which is to say, a truly wise heart? How do we count our days so that we may access the wisdom given to us? Again, imagination is essential. The ability to see possibilities beyond what is right in front of us matters.

Among the writings of the mystics, the work of Caryll Houselander illustrates this in a beautiful teaching. A twentieth-century British woman who was a younger contemporary of Evelyn Underhill and Pierre Teilhard de Chardin, Houselander wrote a wonderful book of meditations on the spirituality of the Virgin Mary called *The Reed of God*. Like many mystics, she emphasizes how Jesus is present in our hearts. Living and writing in the 1940s, she developed an understanding of faith that went beyond the old dualistic way of thinking. To embody God within was not a privilege for those who are "good" or "good Christians." Houselander suggests that Christ is *present* in all people but not necessarily *alive* in all people. We all carry Christ in our hearts, but sometimes we carry the crucified Christ in our hearts as if his body were lying in the tomb the day after he was killed.

Most people know how the story ends. The Christ who died is the Christ who rose again. But for one awful day, the Saturday after the crucifixion, his body lay in repose. Every year, Christians from all over the world travel to Israel to visit the Church of the Holy Sepulchre, built on the site traditionally believed to be the location of Christ's tomb.

Caryll Houselander thought this was ironic. "We should never come to a sinner without the reverence that we would take to the Holy Sepulchre," she wrote. "Pilgrims have travelled on foot for years to kiss the Holy Sepulchre, which is empty. In sinners we can kneel at the tomb in which the dead Christ lies."

Sinner is an archaic word, and many of us are allergic to it because of how some Christians have abused the concept. I think Houselander, as a true mystic, is using this word not to mean those who are outcast because they have been judged unworthy but rather as a humble recognition of a truth that applies to everyone: we all sometimes make choices or commitments that turn us away from love and life. In other words, we all sometimes have stony hearts. Her point: just because you have a stony heart does not mean you have been abandoned by God—or Christ. Even when our hearts need renewal, the divine presence remains within us, even though it may seem buried—as if in a tomb.

The God who is Love-with-a-capital-L is everywhere, which means in all of us. In some, this heavenly presence may be easily recognized, while in others, it remains hidden, like the crucified Christ in repose—and awaiting resurrection. That's the key. Awaiting resurrection. No one is beyond the grace of God. The sooner we recognize this in our hearts, the sooner we are invited into the fullness of joy.

When you encounter someone whose heart seems calcified with hate or bitterness or unapologetic self-ishness, it's easy to assume God has withdrawn from their lives. But Caryll Houselander reminds us that even in these stony hearts, the divine presence rests, waiting for its Easter moment.

So how do we recognize this sacred reality in someone who is hostile to us, or vitriolic, or violent, or acting out an addiction, or in some other way seems to be rejecting the gifts hidden in their heart?

The heart of wisdom says, "Use your imagination."

Imagine Christ in repose in the person's heart, awaiting resurrection. Imagine that a new heart of flesh is being prepared to replace their stony heart. Imagine that miracles can happen at any time, and if you can meet this person—even this angry, hostile person—with an eye to the divine presence deep within, then you become a potential conduit for a miracle rather than just another voice of condemnation.

Our imagination can help us find the divine presence that is hidden everywhere: God in all things.

But this isn't just about our projecting outward. Activating the gift of wisdom means recognizing that we all fall short of the splendor of divine love in so many ways, big and small, each and every day. We are also called to await resurrection within ourselves. *The Book of Common Prayer* succinctly instructs us to confess: "We have not loved you with our whole heart; we have not loved our neighbors as ourselves." Caryll Houselander's insight helps us find Christ in repose in the hearts of difficult people, and we need to apply that same compassion to our own selves. Sometimes Christ sleeps, awaiting resurrection, in our own hearts. Wisdom helps us recognize that divine presence within ourselves, even in our own brokenness and falling-down-ness.

It's not easy. More than one spiritual director has pointed out to me, "You seem to be much more willing to forgive other people than yourself." I suspect I'm not the only one with this problem. Perhaps the gift of wisdom and the fruit of patience have to be turned inward to be most fully realized.

The wisdom in our hearts enables us to forgive others as well as ourselves. It empowers us to find God present even in the worst situations. It gives us the capacity to always imagine a better possibility.

The gift of wisdom can be seen in the beatitude "Blessed are the poor in spirit" (Matthew 5:3). Matthew quotes Jesus in saying the poor *in spirit*. Sometimes we have an interior poverty even when there's money in the bank. Luke's Gospel, meanwhile, records Jesus as simply teaching, "Blessed are you who are poor" (Luke 6:20). Between Matthew and Luke, this beatitude covers all forms of poverty, material as well as spiritual.

To be impoverished implies deprivation—not only the lack of resources but even the lack of choices or possibilities. At its most challenging, to be "poor in spirit" means to feel like you have nowhere to go.

And yet Jesus calls such a person blessed or happy. How can this be?

There's an archetype that shows up in various cultures around the world; the twentieth-century contemplative author Henri Nouwen wrote a book about it: *The Wounded Healer*. Many healers have suffered in some way—an illness or a wound. This wound opens up within them a better capacity to truly heal others due to their own experience and understanding of need. "Blessed are you who are poor" points to a similar type of wounded healer—who knows happiness regardless of their circumstances, who brings healing by helping us recognize inner wisdom and/or the divine presence. This is not to excuse economic injustice or to suggest that poverty is always linked to happiness. Jesus's point is that financial (or any other kind of) stability does not guarantee happiness, and because of the dignity of the human spirit, sometimes those who are deprived are, paradoxically, more spiritually mature—and joyous—than those who cling to their many possessions. The wise one who has known spiritual or physical or financial poverty may be the one who can show us what really matters.

Maybe the poor and poor in spirit are blessed because they can more easily access the wisdom that has been hidden in their hearts. It's not obscured by the noise of other things, the buzz of wealth or material possessions. Those who have discovered their humblest selves—their addicted selves, their impoverished selves, their stony-heart selves—perhaps can more easily find wisdom in the place between the beats of the heart, where they may imagine God's presence and action in their lives and all lives. The urge to judge others may more readily fall away. Spiritual insight and loving knowledge—wisdom—may more readily be manifest.

Rabbi Shneur Zalman of Liadi once said, "There is no thought that can take hold of You," referring to God's transcendental elusiveness. The greatest feat of human wisdom remains incapable of cradling the vastness of the divine presence; our finite minds simply cannot fully receive the infinity of the God who transcends being itself. But—in words that echo the wisdom found in *The Cloud of Unknowing*—this eighteenth-century Hasidic master goes on to point out, "The infinite God is taken hold of by the longing of the heart." In his wonderful book of Jewish mysticism, *Gate to the Heart*, Rabbi Zalman Schachter-Shalomi states, "When the 'longing of the heart' takes over, we are no longer dealing with the God-idea in the third person; we are dealing with the second-person Presence of the living God."

It's easy to know *about* God, as if God were an idea. As John Lennon famously said, "God is a concept by which we measure our pain." No argument there, as far as it goes; for many people, God is nothing more than an idea, a proposition, a story, a sign or symbol. Which explains why it is so easy to get God wrong. Some people turn God into a tool that they use to express aggression or hostility to others: "submit to my God or you are not okay." In its extreme form, this need to control devolves into religiously motivated violence, as seen in troubled places like Palestine or Iraq or Northern Ireland. Others, often recoiling from how God has become a symbol for religious aggression, reject God altogether, seeing the God-concept as a myth, a fairy tale, an example of mushy thinking and emotionally arrested development.

What both fundamentalists and atheists have in common is relating to God-as-concept rather than God-as-living-presence. As another great Jewish thinker, Martin Buber, pointed out, we can relate to other living beings in a face-to-face, presence-to-presence way as "I-Thou," or we can relate to anything we encounter (living or not, sentient or not) as a mere object, making the relationship an "I-It" relationship. When we reduce God to an "it," it's easier to reject God or use God as a tool for aggression. But when we settle into that place of infinite longing in our hearts, all our mind-generated attempts to control the concept of God no longer have much power or meaning, and we are more capable of encountering, in sacred silence, the unspeakable, transrational Presence of God—the ultimate "Thou" who is also an "I" who meets *us* as "thou."

> Those who have discovered their humblest selves—their addicted selves, their impoverished selves, their stony-heart selves—perhaps can more easily find wisdom in the place between the beats of the heart.

If we gaze into the face of God, silence becomes the only appropriate response—the only adequate conductor of love responding to Love. Words fail us. Concepts break down under the divine effulgence. And at the last, we recognize that the heart of true wisdom, the wisdom given to us in our hearts, is nothing we can comprehend or cleverly put into words. Oh, yes, we will try. We will give our lives to trying feebly to articulate that which cannot be spoken. All the while, though, the heart will long for the One who meets our garbled language with infinite, wordless compassion. And there, in the silence between the beats, as we receive the gifts of patience and growing wisdom, in the sinews where wisdom meets patience, wisdom opens the heart for love, peace, and joy.

Heart Practice:
Hospitality

"All guests who present themselves are to be welcomed as Christ, for he himself will say: I was a stranger and you welcomed me." With these words, Benedict instructed monks on how they were to approach a central feature of monastic spirituality: the reception of guests. Hospitality means caring for people's most intimate needs: giving exhausted travelers a place to rest, serving good food to those who hunger, and providing other resources as necessary. And as my story about traveling with my disabled daughter illustrates, many people who rely on the hospitality of others bring special or extraordinary needs far beyond just their famished, weary bodies. To be a person of hospitality means to be one who welcomes both friend and stranger into the sanctuary of one's life.

If you're not a monk or a bed-and-breakfast proprietor, perhaps you may only occasionally welcome a family member or college buddy into the physical sanctuary of your home. Spiritually speaking, it may well be that to practice hospitality, we must welcome guests into our hearts at least as often, if not more so, as we welcome strangers into our homes. For some of us, opening our hearts may prove to be even more challenging than opening our front doors. Yet if we adopt Benedict's perspective, we find the practice of spiritual hospitality means recognizing Christ—the divine presence—in all people, therefore welcoming them into our lives the way we would welcome Jesus (or the Buddha, or whomever our most cherished spiritual guide might be).

As I write these words, I know that hospitality necessarily looks different for different people. The spiritual practice of hospitality is not meant to be a form of harmful self-denial. A person who has been traumatized or victimized might simply need to guard their heart rather than risk inviting a stranger in, which in the wrong circumstances might feel unsafe or even cause further trauma. And hospitality should not come at the expense of those who already rely on my care—since I must ensure that my family, my children, and others who depend on me remain safe and cared for, what if welcoming all guests as Christ could overtax me emotionally or materially? Is it wise to devote too much time to caring for others—to the point where I might even be neglecting those who count on me the most?

These questions point to a simple but challenging fact: hospitality is messy. Inviting a tired traveler into our homes—or an upset friend into our hearts—always entails a matter of risk. The guest could take advantage of me, steal from me, or even hurt me. Spiritual hospitality has no policy manual. What might seem a safe risk for me could be totally earth-shattering for you. We each must be discerning about what we can (or cannot) do to receive others as if we were receiving Christ. Hospitality requires good boundaries to be a healthy and responsible practice.

Perhaps the practice of hospitality begins with a basic attitude that says I can trust the Spirit, I can trust myself, and I can trust life. Because of that trust, I can be generous to those who enter my life in need. How generous or how often—that's up for discernment. But if I ground my hospitality in trust rather than in self-protection, I will discern how to welcome Christ faithfully, even if prudently.

Hospitality comes naturally to some people, and if that's you, keep on keepin' on. If you are like me and tend to be as parsimonious with your time and energy as you are with your money or your home, the spiritual call to hospitality might best be answered with baby steps. Can you give one hour to someone in need next week—listening to a distraught coworker, talking to a homeless person, or calling a lonely shut-in to simply listen as they chat?

Hospitality essentially means being receptive (Jesus's words "you welcomed me" implies how I may respond when another approaches me), so it might even begin with simply a commitment to considering ways to be more open, flexible, and welcoming whenever anyone interrupts the normal flow of your routine with an unexpected need. No one is required to solve the world's problems, but everyone can be a conduit for kindness and grace to those in need, even if ultimately, we must refer them to someone else. As we learn to be more generous with that kindness and grace, even if only in small ways, we create space in our hearts for blessings to flow—to us, and through us.

6

LOVE

I know precious little about my ancestry. My surname, McColman, is associated with the Scottish Clan Buchanan. I've only been to Scotland once, but there's so much I love about my Celtic heritage. I have a responsible but affectionate relationship with whisky, and the sound of bagpipes could almost turn this pacifist into a pugilist. I wore my kilt when Fran and I got married and when we renewed our vows twelve years later upon becoming Catholic (the Buchanans were Jacobites, and many of the Jacobites were Catholic, so I come by that honestly as well).

But perhaps nothing is more ingrained into my Scottish identity than my rather hardwired aversion to spending money—or even to sharing it.

Generosity simply didn't seem to be a word in our family vocabulary. I remember as a child hearing my dad joke about how a good Scotsman always figures out how to disappear when it's his turn to buy a round of drinks. I understand that ethnic and cultural stereotypes are always problematic and can sometimes lead to bigotry and prejudice; my point here is neither to make fun of my people and heritage nor to imply that my own parsimony can just be chalked up to my DNA. For whatever reason, I have a Scottish last name and a decidedly tight-fisted relationship to lucre, filthy or otherwise.

But even the stoniest of hearts can be given new life—as we've already seen. In my case, that means even the most miserly of hearts (Gaelic or otherwise) might discover the ways of generosity. And that's exactly what has happened to me, so let me tell you a story about how I learned to have a more trusting relationship with money.

As Rhiannon's illness progressed, she frequently needed to visit the doctor for checkups or for blood transfusions. At times, her blood counts could drop to life-threatening levels, and then she would have to spend several nights in the hospital to get her anemia under control. As Rhiannon's primary caregiver, Fran spent many hours in waiting rooms or by the bed. Given the stress of doctor visits or long hospital stays, she found she needed a creative outlet that was both nurturing and calming to sustain her. She discovered a calligraphy method called Zentangle, which involves using pen and ink to create beautiful images using simple, repetitive patterns. From the first time she encountered it, Fran loved this meditative practice and soon was filling up sketchpads with various "tangles" or patterns she learned online or from the Zentangle classes she took at the local Episcopal cathedral.

When Rhiannon entered hospice, both Fran and I took time off from work to care for her, which created a measure of financial limitation for us. We had to watch our pennies and be frugal, particularly with unnecessary expenses (a situation where my "Scottishness" came in handy). In those challenging days, Fran confided in me that she drew so much solace and joy from her Zentangle drawings that as she thought about what the future might hold, she dreamed of becoming a certified Zentangle instructor, which would involve traveling to Rhode Island (where the Zentangle creators lived) and participating in a training workshop.

After Rhiannon's funeral, I looked into this, thinking it would be a wonderful gift to give Fran. Unfortunately, it was expensive, and we simply didn't have the money to justify both the tuition for the course and the travel expense.

This was the fall of 2014, and somebody—bless them, I don't recall who—suggested I look into crowdfunding, the practice of using a website to tell a person's story and raise money to either pay for medical bills or otherwise assist them in a time of need. So I signed up for a GoFundMe account and invited people to help Fran get her Zentangle training.

Within a month, we had all the money we needed to pay for the entire trip—travel *and* tuition. I was stunned. It was almost as if the entire thing were magic. Indeed, the money raised was just enough to cover the expenses and the GoFundMe fees.

The average amount given by each donor was about $30. Granted, most of the people who pitched in were family and friends, but there were a few folks whose names I didn't recognize. Plenty of people only gave $5 or $10, but others gave more. One altruistic soul pitched in $1,000. But it all added up to help a grieving mom make at least one dream come true.

Having stinginess hardwired into my personality, I tend to assume everyone else is as tight-fisted as I am. Even while setting up the GoFundMe page, my inner critic kept saying, "Why would people give? It's not like she *needs* to be a Zentangle teacher! There are lots of people whose needs are more serious!" But in telling this story, I left out one little detail: When I set the crowdfunding page up, I made a promise to myself and to God. I made a commitment that I would find a way to cover whatever expenses that crowdfunding didn't cover. Without any fuss, I made an interior commitment to be generous for the sake of my bereaved wife, even though at the time, I had no idea where the money would be coming from. Stepping out on faith, I then humbly asked others to pitch in. And they did, beyond my wildest imagination.

As Fran excitedly planned her trip, I came away from this experience with a sense of profound humility—and a newfound appreciation for what really *is* possible when we approach life from a position of generosity rather than miserliness.

I wish I could say I've been nothing but generous ever since. It's more accurate to say that I became a learner of generosity who still falls down on occasion. My stony-to-flesh heart transplant seems to be an ongoing process. Old habits die hard, and I have to remind myself to be a more giving person. But I can find the generosity in me whenever I remember how lots of people made relatively small gifts and it all added up to one wonderful blessing—all for someone I love so very much.

Love. That's what I discerned at the heart of this. Love made me willing to step out of the prison of my own ungenerosity, love gave me the humility to ask others for help, and love then inspired the dozens of friends, family, and even strangers to respond with such kindness, compassion, and largesse. My Wiccan friends like to say, "Love is the greatest magic." In Christianity, we tend to talk about miracles instead of magic, but I

> **Love is the greatest magic. Love is the greatest miracle.**

think we could easily reply, "Love is the greatest miracle." Not only is love a miracle in itself; it makes countless other miracles possible.

The experience of falling in love can create a fluttering feeling in the chest, so it's no wonder that we have come to believe that love resides in our hearts. It is no surprise that the apostle Paul in his letter to the Romans identifies love as a gift given to us in our hearts: "Hope does not disappoint us, because God's love has been poured into our hearts through the Holy Spirit that has been given to us" (Romans 5:5). Love poured into our hearts—but more than just ordinary human love (as beautiful as that may be). The love that has been so generously given to our hearts is divine love, the love of God. This love makes it possible to have hope no matter how difficult or challenging life's circumstances might be.

Our hearts are the chalices in which the wine of divine love has been poured. We can sense this intuitively whenever we have found ourselves in love, or expressing love, or even responding to the love of another. The human heart is calibrated to give and receive human love simply because it is the repository of divine love: "We love because God first loved us" (1 John 4:19). When we recognize and celebrate this promise of the heart, we find the power within us not only to be more compassionate, kind, and caring but also to access deep and lasting joy.

Take a moment to contemplate this with me: You already contain, in your heart, the love of God. Whether you feel it or not, it's there; whether you allow it to guide your life or not, it's available to you. You didn't have to earn it, or prove it, or show yourself worthy. It is a gift, simply given. The question is not "Do I get it?" but rather "What do I do with it?" How do we allow the love in our hearts to emerge and shape and direct our lives?

Our hearts are the chalices in which the wine of divine love has been poured.

Like all the gifts of the heart, divine love is not contingent on knowing the right secret, performing the correct ritual, or adhering to the proper doctrine. Sure, there are great resources of wisdom, powerful teachings, and meaningful ceremonies and sacraments that are well worth exploring in any of the world's great sacred traditions. But the promises of the heart are more universal, more foundational, than any spiritual system or religious dogma. We find these promises echoed in all the world's great traditions—because they point to our universal birthright as human beings.

Love is not only a gift of the heart; it is also a fruit of the Spirit. Think of it as a "firstfruit," for it is the first of the nine fruits of the Spirit that Paul spells out in Galatians 5:22–23. It is the firstfruit of the mystical qualities, virtues, and characteristics that manifest in the lives of all who calibrate their hearts to resonate with the divine presence given to us—not by virtue of our religious identity, sacramental status, moral worthiness, or acceptance of any particular creed but simply by virtue of being human.

This heavenly Spirit, who by virtue of being everywhere naturally resides in our hearts, is necessary for our very existence. But even though the Spirit has been given to us, this does not necessarily mean that we automatically manifest the firstfruit of divine love. That takes a willingness to accept and receive the gifts that have been given. The grace (gift) of love is free. We have a choice as to how we receive and respond to such grace.

In the famous love chapter of Paul's first letter to the Corinthians, love is called the greatest of God's gifts to us (1 Corinthians 13:13). I often think of Love as pure light, a luminous ray that contains all the colors of the rainbow. Receiving this light, the heart—at least, the heart attuned to the leading of the Spirit—functions as a prism, and the various fruits of the Spirit are like the colors of the rainbow, refracted out of the love poured into our hearts by the Spirit.

The French philosopher Jean-Luc Marion wrote a fascinating book called *God Without Being*. In it, he explores the difference between idols and icons—icons in the spiritual sense, such as what are found in an Orthodox church (a visual depiction of Christ, or the Trinity, or any of the saints or angels). As Marion points out, icons and idols have a fundamental difference: an idol is anything that is not-God but that is worshipped as if it were a god. In our day, examples of such "idols" could include money, or security, or glamour, or power (real or imagined). Such things can be abused when we place all our hope and meaning and trust in them. They can become spiritual black holes that distract us from the radical freedom that comes from worshiping God alone—the God who is Love-with-a-capital-L, the undefinable God who is limitless love and unbounded compassion. Placing our trust in a false god like money or security only leads back to existential restlessness— the restlessness that only the unbounded love of the divine can cure.

Icons, unlike idols, function more like a telephone or other communications device. When you hand your phone to your three-year-old and say, "It's Grandma; here, speak to Grandma," obviously the phone isn't the grandmother. Even the toddler figures this out. But the phone enables us to speak to someone far away in a real manner. This is how icons function. When someone kisses an icon or lights a candle in front of it, they are praying or worshipping *through* the icon to the divine presence hidden beyond it. When we talk about the love of God poured into our hearts, we are, in effect, saying that each one of us can function as a "living icon" of divine love.

Even deeper and more precious than the beautiful, sacred images we might find in a church or monastery, you and I are icons of divine love. We may not always act as such and likely have a hard time seeing it in ourselves. But even the most bitter, angry, traumatized, wounded, and/or self-centered person still has, deep within, the capacity to present love to the world. Remember the wisdom of Caryll Houselander: even if it is hidden deep beneath our wounds or our suffering or the harm we inflict on others (or ourselves), the potential to embody divine love remains within every human being.

God created everyone in the divine image and likeness. God's divine image and likeness persist within all creation, even in people who we think of as broken, abusive, or evil. God's love resides in them no matter how deeply it is buried or hidden. Everyone has the potential, the possibility, of presenting divine love to the world. As we continue along the spiritual path within, the love poured into our hearts invites us to be formed—or, perhaps reformed—into the loving persons we are called to be. We are called to be truly, authentically ourselves—the persons God imagined us to be before the creation of the world, persons born to receive and share love abundantly, lavishly, and generously.

Since the imagination can be such a rich portal into the heart, let's imagine what's possible in response to the gift of love. In our imagination, we can create entire worlds. Such imaginal capacity to create is almost limitless. As the imagination of the mind thinks up ideas that we can choose to conform our lives to (or not), so the imagination of the heart, in harmony with all the gifts that have been placed there by the Spirit, can create new avenues of love—new potentialities for compassion and caring and charity—that can literally revolutionize our world.

Since God is love, when we imagine new possibilities for love, we are, in essence, giving birth to God anew in our hearts. When we imagine new possibilities for

Progressing on our journey along the spiritual path in our hearts, we are called to form ourselves in response to the divine love.

love, we are also acknowledging the heavenly presence within the heart of others. This is the beauty of the traditional Sanskrit greeting, *namaste*—"the divine in me honors the divine in you."

The heart calibrated for love becomes a living icon of Mary's womb; it is the channel by which divine love is born, again and anew, into the world. It is the chalice of compassion, the paten of charity, the font of eros, the altar of agapé. The imagination of the heart is the arena in which the mysteries of Christ continually emerge into our lives and through our lives flow into the world at large. In us, Christ—the incarnation of Love—is born and born again and ever born anew. This is the true Christian mysticism: the mystery of Christ.

This unteachable mystery cannot be passed down, but everyone is capable of realizing and manifesting it. Imagine it, emerging in your heart, out of the ocean of God's silence that flows within you between every heartbeat. This mystery of love emanates out of the silence, and each heartbeat sends it forth—into our minds, into our bodies, into our thoughts and feelings and words and deeds. When we calibrate our lives to the love of God, we become—in the words of John of the Cross—living flames of love.

"The imagination may well be our greatest asset, which helps us break out of modern one-dimensional ways of living, enabling us to engage our multi-dimensional potentials for transformation," wrote psychologist Mick Collins in *The Visionary Spirit.* Our imagination is more than just a capacity to create mental pictures; it is an invitation into an expanding way of seeing, of thinking, of wondering, and of loving. Benedict describes the monastic life as "running with an expanding heart"—running on the path, of course, but with a heart that is growing larger with the ever-increasing love given to it by the Spirit. A physical heart may be in trouble when it gets enlarged, but for the spiritual heart, this is a blessing. As our hearts expand through love, we can imagine these "multi-dimensional potentials for transformation" and live into the possibilities that the adventure of love holds for us.

Life continually changes, and so does the universe, so simply saying that the mystical life involves transformation merely sets the stage for this important question: What kind of transformation does the gift of love call us to? One answer may come from this beatitude: "Blessed are those who hunger and thirst for righteousness, for they will be filled" (Matthew 5:6). What a remarkable promise. Jesus is clearly speaking metaphorically here about a "hunger" not experienced physically. What, exactly, will fill those who hunger for righteousness? Righteousness is not something to feast on; it is a way of living.

What fills the happy person who hungers for righteousness are the "nutrients" necessary to make righteousness manifest. What is the nutrient we need more than anything else to create a world where righteousness is more than just a lofty ideal? Love.

The Spirit promises to fill us with love—provided we then give that love away. If you try to hoard love, it spoils as surely as milk does. We can be misers with money and time and comfort, but love is only real when it continues to flow from God to us, and from us to one another. This is why working to create a righteous world—which is to say, a world of justice, of integrity and authenticity, of societies and relationships based on inclusivity and equality—is essential to any sustained spiritual life. "Let the truth be in your hearts . . . and you will see clearly what love we are bound to have for our neighbors," says Saint Teresa of Ávila in *The Way of Perfection*.

Righteousness can sound like a pious and churchy word. So perhaps we need to unpack it a bit. The Greek word has a connotation more of social justice than of personal moral rectitude. In our day, we clearly see who truly hungers for the social dimensions of justice (and righteousness)—namely, those who suffer because of systemic oppression. This includes not only those who lack access to economic or educational resources but also those whose lives are harmed by racism, sexism, homophobia, transphobia. People who benefit from social privilege sometimes scoff at the idea that such a thing as "social privilege" even exists, but those who lack white privilege or male privilege or straight/cis privilege see it all too clearly.

To hunger for righteousness means to hunger for a world where we all join together to dismantle the social and economic barriers related to systems of privilege. This seems a daunting task, especially given the opposition of those who believe that individuals rather than systems are at fault for the problems in society. Alas, we live in an imperfect world, which means a world where some of our own brothers and sisters, our kin and neighbors, will be deaf to love's call and perhaps even seek to flee its self-giving demands.

"Our hearts are restless." Alas, such restlessness not only manifests in spiritual disquiet but also contributes to our pervasive social conflicts and inequities. This existential restlessness seems to be hardwired into the human condition. But there's always hope. Those who say yes to the call of the Spirit today may well have been the same ones who said no yesterday, which means that those who say no today might say yes tomorrow.

People who either actively oppose efforts to create a more just society or turn a blind eye to the suffering of those who are harmed by systems of privilege or oppression suffer from a kind of spiritual lack. They are among those whose stony hearts have not yet been transformed. Christ remains buried in them, awaiting resurrection at some future date.

Those who truly hunger and thirst for righteousness must find ways to create a better world in spite of the inertia of those who refuse to cooperate and even in spite of those who would oppose them. In this way, the struggle for justice truly becomes an exercise of an expanding heart, filling with increasing dimensions of love that demand to be shared.

Rumi describes God as the One "who keeps the keys to open our hearts." Love is that key: it is only through love that we are given the capacity to meet the world's suffering with openness and the strength to make a difference. Another Sufi poet, Rabia, speaks of how even nature can be our ally: "The sky gave me its heart," she sang, "because it knew mine was not large enough to care for the earth." A heart big enough for love must be bigger than the sky.

Julian of Norwich, in her sixteenth showing, tells of an expanded heart that is indeed greater than the sky: "And then our good lord opened my spiritual eye and showed me my soul, in the middle of my heart. I saw the soul so large as it were an endless world, and a blissful realm, and a shimmering city." The heart that receives the love given to it is in fact receiving its very own soul—and that soul is as big as the world, as big as a shining city. The Irish mystic John O'Donohue said that the soul is not in the body; the body is in the soul. Rather than contradicting Julian, he may be pointing to a profound mystical truth: the soul is in the heart, and the heart is in the body, and the body is in the soul. It's all true—a kind of Möbius strip of divine felicity in which each dimension of our existence cradles love and is cradled in love.

The spiritual heart is bigger on the inside than on the outside thanks to the miracle of love. Heavenly love not only reveals the presence of God but forms the very architecture of the soul. Physically we are beings made of stardust, and spiritually we are beings fashioned of the very love of God. The deeper we move into love, the larger it gets. Every subatomic particle unfolds a universe, and love scales all the way down and all the way up.

If love, the firstfruit of the Spirit, is the pure light from which the colorful lights of all the other fruits are refracted, can any of the other fruits especially be paired with the gift of love? Yes—I believe the fruit of goodness inspires the hunger for righteousness, the blossoming of love, and the ever-expanding heart.

When we meditate on how God pours love into our hearts and then choose to live oriented toward that love, goodness naturally blossoms in our lives. This doesn't necessarily mean we become Goody Two-shoes; goodness is far different from just a kind of puerile, smug self-righteousness. That is just a type of moral hubris, and we don't have to confuse it with the luminous, life-giving freedom of authentic spiritual goodness.

So how do we manifest that deep, authentic goodness? It is always distilled from love—not from pride, not from a fawning desire to please, not from a kind of masochistic self-abnegation in order to curry favor with someone in power. Being distilled from love, one way to understand goodness would be to use the same language the apostle Paul uses to describe love in 1 Corinthians 13. Goodness, therefore, is patient; goodness is kind; goodness is not envious or boastful or arrogant or rude. Goodness does not insist on its own way; it is not irritable or resentful; it does not rejoice in wrongdoing, but rejoices in the truth. Goodness bears all things, believes all things, hopes all things, endures all things.

There is a basic humility and unassuming quality to manifesting the goodness of love. It's the art of finding quiet delight in choosing what is healthy and caring and compassionate. It understands that forgiveness matters even in the midst of furious anger. It means being willing to make the unpopular choice just because it is the right thing to do, so there is real courage in goodness as well. Goodness is not passively allowing others to take advantage of us, but it also takes no comfort in revenge and sees holding grudges as pointless. Goodness is mature, conscious, healthy, serene. It's attractive in a quiet and nonglamourous sort of way. Since goodness is distilled from love, we can look for goodness as a sign that we are giving the love in our hearts free and generous rein in our lives.

We can no more force goodness to emerge in our lives than we can force love or any of the other fruits of the Spirit—or gifts of the heart—to manifest. But if you cultivate love in your heart, don't be surprised when one day, someone says, "You're different . . ." and what they go on to say sounds like a description of goodness itself. That's when you'll know that the blossom is beginning to open.

Heart Practice:
Generosity

Like hospitality, the practice of generosity is relational; to give requires someone to receive. One way to define generosity is "serving others with gladness and good cheer." It's not just the giving that makes one generous but the capacity to give in a way that is shaped by love.

Generosity, like any dimension of goodness, flows most beautifully and joyfully when it emerges spontaneously and without fuss from our hearts. As I learned from my own lack of generosity, God giving us a new heart to replace the old stony heart is not a once-and-done operation. We have a tendency to (re)turn to stone, to refuse the gifts given to us, and then we have to remember and try—get up—again.

If you are more like me than like Mother Teresa, take courage. Allowing generosity to flow into your life might have to begin as an intentional act—at least at first, and maybe forever. It's really an extension and a deepening of hospitality. Hospitality is generosity with our time and our space, a willingness to invite the stranger even into our homes. Generosity responds to another person's need in whatever form it takes, welcoming them to share our abundance.

Just as there are many ways to practice hospitality, generosity likewise takes many forms. What makes a spiritual practice like this most beneficial, and most conducive to vibrant interior growth, is finding that amount or type of generosity that stretches you, even if just a little bit. Find that stretchy place and then lean into it.

This might mean you have to learn to perform a small act of generosity as an ongoing practice. Write a check to the Red Cross or the United Way. Make a pledge to your local public broadcasting service. Or the next time you encounter a homeless person, offer to buy them dinner—and have a conversation with them while they eat.

Generosity encompasses more than just a willingness to share your money, important as that often may be. Generosity can mean not only sharing our resources but also largesse with our talents, our time, our patience and forbearance, and even our attachment to comfort and control. People who are uncomfortable with sharing freely in one area might find it easier to be generous in another. Don't be too hard on yourself when considering all the ways you fail to be generous—and likewise, don't rest on your laurels when reflecting on the generosities that come more easily to you. Offer thanks to God for the ways you already are willing to share with others and humbly ask for the ability to stretch spiritually in order to share other dimensions of your life more freely and self-forgetfully.

Hospitality and generosity form a kind of yin-yang of sharing. With hospitality, we express love by receiving others who are weary or suffering and aim to help them by our welcoming. Generosity is more outward-focused:

we love by reaching out to others out of our abundance, freely giving so that somehow, we might bless another person. Sharing is the common ingredient here. It's important to remember that we can only give out of our abundance: "We love because God first loved us." We give so freely because we have so freely and fully received. Now it's time to pass it on, to pay it forward.

7

ETERNITY

Mystical Christianity—and mysticism in general—first came to me by means of the written word. Through my adolescent and young adult years, I discovered the beckoning of eternity in the poetry of William Blake, the spiritual nonfiction of Evelyn Underhill, the depth psychology of Morton Kelsey, and even the wisdom teachings from other traditions as disclosed by Paramahansa Yogananda and Alan Watts.

But there's more to mysticism—and to spirituality in general—than just reading what others have to say about the topic. Someone once told me that reading about prayer is one of our favorite ways to avoid actually praying. I love how words and writing can inspire the imagination and invite us into new worlds of inner wonder, but I agree: the words ultimately point us to a place beyond words. We need to follow where they lead us—and beyond.

If we authentically wish to enter into the mysteries of the interior or hidden life, we need to do something to make that desire real, to embody it in our lives. What this usually means is adopting spiritual practices—exercises or disciplines designed to foster or deepen our awareness of or connection to the Spirit. Most of these spiritual practices are universal (prayer, meditation, contemplation, self-discipline, hospitality, generosity, chanting, fasting) and can be found, in slightly different forms, within different religious and spiritual traditions the world over.

Over the years, I have explored a variety of such practices within Christianity and other traditions, including the Jesus Prayer, Centering Prayer, mindfulness meditation, shamatha meditation, and zazen (Zen meditation). Meditative and contemplative exercises such as following my breath, repeating a prayer word, and gently learning to allow distracting thoughts to come and go have been both meaningful and insightful as I have tried to embody a more spiritual life over the years.

When it comes to the practices associated with the spiritual life, I've discovered that some exercises I love more than others. I wish I could say I have meditated my way into enlightenment—or at least sainthood. But the truth is hardly exciting; I remain a mere mortal, clumsy and imperfect and prone to getting grouchy when hungry or tired. Like a fussy kid who craves hamburgers but has no use for peas, I've discovered that I am far less enthusiastic about some of the less glamorous spiritual practices, such as praying the Liturgy of the Hours (also known as the Divine Office or the Daily Office). If you're new to these terms, they refer to the practice, found especially among monks and nuns, of chanting or reciting an established set of prayers, psalms, and canticles several times each day. These prayers are compiled in books known as breviaries.

If you invited me to deepen my breath, relax, and practice a discipline of letting go of my thoughts so I could be still and know God, I'd probably say, "When do we start?" But when it comes to gathering with other people to pray from a breviary (or even picking up the breviary by myself and praying in solitude), I have a much harder time working up the enthusiasm. Reciting printed prayers out of a book, day after day after day? It seems so formulaic, so repetitive, so . . . *rote*! How could this be spiritually formative?

Getting to know contemplative practitioners from other faiths, however, has forced me to reevaluate my bias against such recited prayers. First, I became friends with a Sufi Muslim who prayed five times a day, no matter what, typically reciting the same passages from the Qur'an day in and day out. Later, I spent some time meditating daily with a group of Buddhists who began their morning meditation with the same few chants—again, day in and day out. They had other chants for the evening that were just as formulaic, involving the same words each and every day. I began to wonder if I were spoiled. At least the Christian liturgy changed from day to day based on the readings and whether it was Lent or Easter or some other time of the year.

But I'm nothing if not obstinate. I continued to question why such repetitive praying mattered. Why do it? Why pray out of a book? Even if the Liturgy of the Hours doesn't use the exact same words from day to day, it nevertheless does follow a rhythm, and over time you repeat the cycles and keep praying the same words over and over. What's the point?

There are plenty of good reasons for giving ourselves generously to this way of praying. Among other things, the Divine Office provides us with a language for prayer, teaches us who God is (and who we are in response to God), and helps form our identity as people of prayer.

And then one day, I read one of the loveliest descriptions of the spiritual beauty of routine, liturgical prayer. An Anglican Benedictine monk, Father Aidan Owen, OHC, is the Guestmaster of Holy Cross Monastery in West Park, New York. Occasionally he sends out email newsletters to friends of the monastery, and in one such missive, he mused on the purpose behind the daily practice of monks praying the Psalms and other Scripture passages:

> I'm reminded of a conversation I had with Br. Ron before I entered the Monastery. I asked him what it was like to pray the Office day in and day out for over forty years, worrying, I suppose, that it must get a bit boring. He surprised and delighted me by saying that it was like staring out into eternity. There is so much space and no hurry at all. . . . Each time we pray the Office or celebrate the Eucharist or sit in silent prayer, we return to eternity, where God always lives, and we allow God to remind us that God's peace and justice and love are already right here and right now, even as they are not fully visible or manifest.

Reading that, my imagination began to glow. If even rote prayer can be "like staring out into eternity," that's a way of saying that ordinary daily prayers—even the same words that some people have been offering to God for years on end—can usher us beyond the confines of time itself.

Not that eternity is some faraway place; on the contrary, it is closer to us than we are to ourselves. The beauty of daily prayers—even when recited from a book—is that they can remind us of what is already here and now, and they help us see what is right in front of our noses (and in our hearts) even though we all too often fail to notice such immediate blessings. They can help us see from a new perspective.

"Rituals are part of every culture," notes the Wiccan priestess Starhawk. "They are the events that bind a culture together, that create a heart, a center, for a people. It is ritual that evokes the Deep Self of a group. In ritual (a patterned movement of energy to accomplish a purpose) we become familiar with power-from-within, learn to recognize its feel, learn how to call it up and let it go."

The Christian word for daily prayers, *liturgy*, carries a meaning similar to what Starhawk means by ritual. It comes from a couple of Greek words that mean "the work of the people." The prefix, *lit-*, is related to the word *laity*, meaning "people," while *-urgy* is related to the same root that gave us *ergonomics* or *energy*, meaning "work." So liturgy is laity-energy: the work of people seeking to create a closer spiritual bond with God.

Whether you call it liturgy, or fixed-hour prayer, or the Divine Office, it's prayer in ritual form. It's a spiritual practice that enables communities such as monasteries or small groups in churches to easily pray together—that's the "people" part—and like almost any other ritual, we can also pray this way when we're alone. Spiritually speaking, when we pray a shared prayer like the Liturgy of the Hours, we are never really alone, even if we pray in solitude. Our prayers join with others from around the world in a shared song of adoration, supplication, and gratitude.

The Psalms, sublime and transformational prayers when chanted in a community, can work their magic in solitude just as well. As we move farther along the path of the heart, we are called into more sustainable and meaningful forms of community while simultaneously being called deeper into the desert of radical aloneness. Both communal and solitary ways of prayer can open us up to the gift of eternity—for eternity is more than just an abstract, far-off reality; it is yet another gift already given, a gift found in our hearts.

> When we pray a shared prayer like the Liturgy of the Hours, we are never really alone, even if we pray in solitude. Our prayers join with others from around the world in a shared song of adoration, supplication, and gratitude.

One of the most fascinating books of the Old Testament, Ecclesiastes, is a deeply existential text of philosophical musings. Traditionally thought to be the writing of King Solomon, most scholars today see it as a spiritual literary masterpiece from an anonymous source. In the Bible, Ecclesiastes is grouped with other writings like Job, the Psalms, Proverbs, and the Song of Songs—collectively known as the "Wisdom Books," for they consist not of historical narrative or prophetic utterances but rather of poetry and poetic prose, offering reflective insights into many aspects of life's meaning, from the beauty of love, to the problem of suffering, to words of worship for God, to moral precepts for an ethical life.

Among the wisdom writings, Ecclesiastes is remarkable because of its ambiguity. In places it seems surprisingly pessimistic for a book of spiritual wisdom: "All is vanity . . . all things are wearisome . . . there is nothing new under the sun." Whoever this philosopher was, they certainly had a shadow side and were not afraid to express it.

Living as we do in such a profoundly cynical time as our twenty-first century, the philosophy of Ecclesiastes might be easier for some people to accept than many of the ideas found in other biblical books, filled as they are with mythology, the minutiae of ancient history, and arcane religious rules. Take, for example, Ecclesiastes 8:15, from which we get the proverb "Eat, drink, and be merry." Here the author suggests that since no human being can ever fully know for sure what it means to be good and righteous, perhaps at the end of the day, it makes the most sense to simply enjoy the life you've been given.

The third chapter of Ecclesiastes starts with the famous poem that beings, "For everything there is a season, and a time for every matter under heaven"— immortalized in the song "Turn! Turn! Turn!" written by Pete Seeger and made a hit by the sixties folk-rock group the Byrds. Following that poem, the author of Ecclesiastes indulges in a bit of existential humility, musing on how little human beings can know of the mind and purposes of God. In the middle of that meditation, however, the writer makes this bold, profound claim: "[God] has made everything beautiful in its time. He has also set eternity in the human heart; yet no one can fathom what God has done from beginning to end" (Ecclesiastes 3:11).

This is from the New International Version; among different English Bible versions, *eternity* is also translated as "the timeless" or "a sense of past and future" or even an "enigma." The Hebrew word used here is עוֹלָם, *olam*. God has put *olam* into our hearts. But what does this mean? *Olam* evokes a sense of eternity, perpetuity—the quality of forever, always. It's a word that invites us away from time as a linear progression from past to present to future; that linear sense of time is mentioned earlier in the verse: "God has made everything beautiful in its (appointed) time." The relationship between time and eternity functions

> There is always the possibility that something simple will happen today or tomorrow or sometime in the future—and the entire universe will change.

like the relationship between typeset letters and the page on which the letters are printed. Eternity is not just time extended out in a line that never ends; eternity is the page on which the line of chronological time is printed. That is what God has placed in our hearts.

But *olam* carries another shade of meaning as well. It points to a sense of "the cosmos" or "the world." In Jewish spirituality, the phrase *tikkun olam* means, literally, "repairing (or perfecting) the world"—implying that the spiritual work of good people, who observe the teachings and directives of God, is not just a matter of personal morality but truly a matter of social justice as well. *Tikkun olam*: repairing the world, perfecting the cosmos, manifesting eternity . . . maybe even embodying the space-time continuum.

Here's what that old existentialist who wrote Ecclesiastes seems to be saying: *You contain eternity in your heart. You contain the cosmos in your heart. Your heart is a vessel that holds all things as given to us by God.*

For some, this can be profoundly disorienting. "But you don't know *my* heart," someone might object. "My heart is filled with chaos and disorder; the deeper I go, the noisier it gets. The deeper I go, the more chaotic it gets."

Here we are bumping into another paradox at the heart of the spiritual life. The divine presence is everywhere, and yet so often, we experience God only in a sense of absence. God's wisdom, God's law, and indeed, God's new life are all poured into our hearts, and yet we spend much of our lives searching for love in all the wrong places, rejecting the simple message of gentle peace and calm compassion in favor of the fashion and fad of the moment. And even when we are willing to just go with this revolutionary notion—that love and eternity are already present in our hearts—we stand at the threshold of transformation and all too often find some reason to say "No thank you; I really don't want to be a bother" or perhaps "I really don't want to be bothered."

We never blow our trip forever. We fall down, and we get back up. For today we may refuse the invitation to manifest divine love, the call to generosity, the mandate to rebuild our broken world—but then someday, we just might be inspired to welcome the divine presence lying dormant within. There is always the possibility that something simple will happen today or tomorrow or sometime in the future—and the entire universe will change.

On May 24, 1738, a young John Wesley—who would go on to be renowned as the founder of the Methodist denomination of Christianity—was struggling to understand his relationship with God. He attended a religious service in London that spring evening, and as the preacher described the ways in which "God works in the heart through faith in Christ," Wesley had a surprisingly visceral response. He later described that moment: "I felt my heart strangely warmed."

He wrote, "I felt I did trust in Christ, Christ alone for salvation; and an assurance was given me that He had taken away my sins." Whether you resonate with

Wesley's traditional religious language or it seems like a foreign tongue to you, consider what happened in the years that followed. That strangely warmed heart went on to touch thousands of other hearts. That one heart, awakened to the energy of the Spirit, eventually led to countless other hearts "strangely warmed"—warmed by the love of God and inspired to bring love to others through efforts to fight injustice and help those in need. We are always at the threshold of transformation, and we never know just how radically better things could get in the blink of an eye.

The cynic might retort, "Yes, and just as quickly things could get really bad," to which I can only reply, "I fall down and get back up." This spiritual principle applies to epochs and eons as surely as it does to minutes and seconds. Today's tragedy is always a prelude to the possibilities of tomorrow's miracle.

If eternity is in our hearts, then in each moment, we can create a universe with the choices we make. We can create possibilities filled with grace and jubilation and the leisure of eternity, possibilities of renewal that may take a million years and yet always point us back to the now of divine presence—the heart's chalice of wisdom and love, filled to the brim and ready to be shared without reservation with the world. Or we can retreat into fear and suspicion, the cynicism that refuses to trust and is always on the lookout for the catch. It's your life you are creating. What do you want it to be?

I imagine most of us veer between both of these scenarios. Our choices are rarely pure. But even our greatest imperfections are met with the infinite purity of love, and our half-hearted gesture might be all that it would take to create the room for the Holy Spirit to create even more unimagined blessings.

The night John Wesley had his heart strangely warmed came after his disastrous voyage to the American colony of Georgia, where his efforts as a missionary were mired by both interpersonal and institutional conflicts. He fell down, and he got back up.

> **Today's tragedy is always a prelude to the possibilities of tomorrow's miracle.**

Sometimes we make choices that diminish love rather than set it free. When that happens, we can always choose again; we can redirect our path. The African American mystic Thea Bowman observed, "If I hate, the hate eats into my heart and eats into my soul." These are strong words of warning, but the opposite is just as true: whenever I give myself to love, my soul takes flight.

Every choice can diminish our soul or open it to endless light. Don't let this lock you in a paralysis of fear. You have eternity in your heart. You can take your time to say yes to love. Take your time when it comes to choosing life. Take your time when it comes to calibrating your heart and mind to the splendor of heaven and the leisure of eternity. Take your time, for you have all the time in the world. Even if you are on your deathbed, even if you are 105 years old and you understand that far more days stretch out behind you than ahead of you. Our bodies will die, and for most of us, it will feel too soon when it happens. But your heart, your eternal heart, filled as it is with wisdom and love and imagination, knows no such urgency. Saint Makarios of Egypt said, "The heart is a small vessel, but all things are contained in it; God is there, the angels are there, and there also is life and the Kingdom, the heavenly cities and the treasures of grace." Why feel rushed when the very eternal reign of God awaits us in our hearts?

Some true believers will reply, "But the Bible teaches you must accept Jesus before you die, *or else!*" Such thinking is like a drug, stimulating a shot of adrenaline with a frisson of fear. It also represents a fundamental misunderstanding of the teachings of Jesus. Christ always calls us into the present moment; there is no other place where we may fully receive the gifts of love, of life, of transformation, of exaltation, of unitive consciousness. It only happens now. Not tomorrow, not next week, not whenever. So the invitation is always urgent in that kind of ticking-clock sense. But with the gift of eternity in our hearts, the ever-present now is always in us. Even after we die. When we say no to a gift, we miss out; the present is left unopened. But that is not about divine wrath so much as it's just another falling down. And what do we do after we fall down? We get back up.

Always.

The beatitude that tracks most closely with the gift of eternity proclaims, "Blessed are the merciful, for they will receive mercy" (Matthew 5:7). In every act or expression or manifestation of mercy, we may find something of eternity. Mercy pops us out of clock time and into eternity, even if only for a nanosecond. We taste eternity when we give mercy, and we taste it when we receive it. Jesus never describes where mercy comes from. Presumably, it comes from God: "Forgive us our trespasses as we forgive those who trespass against us." But mercy and eternity don't function in any kind of transactional way. God doesn't figure out how much mercy we deserve by tracking how merciful we are to others. The mercy we receive always precedes the mercy we share. It is in the sharing of it that we open our hearts to receive the gift that has already been given and is always there. To quote Thea Bowman again—she's speaking about faith, but her words apply equally well to mercy—"If you sit there and keep your faith locked up in your heart, it's not going to help any."

Some people consider mercy and forgiveness controversial. The bigger the whatever-it-is that needs forgiving, the more controversial mercy becomes. When a convicted murderer gets sentenced to life in prison rather than the death penalty, some react with anger. And people who survive horrible abuse or who have suffered under systemic evils like racism or sexism or homophobia often feel that forgiveness talk is just further victimization. Perhaps they have a point. Mercy and forgiveness belong to eternity, which means sometimes they don't operate according to our human systems of time. It can take a long time to forgive, a long time to be merciful. I think we need to be gentle with this reality. The wisdom of the heart says, "Allow for the eventual possibility of forgiveness and mercy. In the meantime, create the space in your heart where God can do the deep work of inner transformation."

Perhaps by creating space within for God to do that kind of work, we can discover a fruit of the Spirit that likewise makes room for eternity to touch us here and now—the fruit of peace. Peace and eternity seem to go together like wisdom and patience. In my imagination, I find it easy to visualize eternity as embodying deep serenity. Of course, just as I sometimes feel like I have no time and am constantly rushing about, I also often feel like my life lacks genuine peace and quiet.

The fruits of the Spirit represent blessings that can manifest in our lives, where before they may have been absent. In other words, no one is necessarily born with an innate disposition toward patience and kindness and peace. Yes, some people exhibit these eternal qualities even from early childhood. To such persons, I bow in admiration. But for the rest of us mere mortals, a spiritual fruit like peace matters precisely because of how it can arise in our hearts—even when our hearts are anything but peaceful.

Anyone who has ever tried to meditate (or practice any other type of mindfulness exercise) quickly becomes humbled by how unruly and undisciplined their mind seems to be. "I can't meditate," many proclaim in frustration, "because I can't get my head to shut up!" It's a universal problem. The twentieth-century English theologian Kenneth Leech remarked that contemplation challenges us to face "the waste of our own being." This is not a physical waste, like the body produces, but a mental or emotional or spiritual waste that seems to be endlessly dynamic, or distracted, or agitated. Anything but peaceful.

And yet, it is precisely out of the inner noisiness that inner peace might truly arise. Peace is a gift given and received in the midst of conflict. Two countries that have never fought have no need to sign a peace accord. True peace emerges from conflict the same way that adulthood emerges from adolescence. Peace is not a solitary fruit; it is always the sign and sacrament of reconciliation and relationships built or repaired, holding something of the eternal, because it holds that which is divine. Even inner peace has a relational quality: we find inner peace when we reconcile with God and with our own selves. Peace is not merely the absence of conflict any more than silence is merely the absence of noise.

As silence marks the presence of the hidden face of God, so too does peace mark the emergence of reconciliation and relationship as the sign of something new, be it a new hope, a new bond, or a new arena where all the fruits of the Spirit—including love and joy—might freely emerge.

If you feel as if peace is woefully absent from your life and heart, pray for the gift of hope. If you find your attempts to "be still and know God" to be sabotaged by a lack of peace in your mind and heart, try to meet this circumstance with gentleness and self-acceptance. Peace, the fruit of eternity, is not a static state so much as a dynamic quality that invites us into new possibilities and potentialities. Thich Nhat Hanh encourages us to *be* peace and proclaims, "Peace is every step." It's not something static; rather, it is a process, a journey, a pilgrimage. As the first gift of the heart is a path, so peace is the unexpected delight that emerges along the way, just as surely as the sun emerges slowly in each new dawn. Imagine peace emerging in your heart and pray that the process might be something you consciously recognize—an occasion for joy. For the gift of eternity and the fruit of peace bring us to the threshold of joy.

Heart Practice:
Liturgy, the Poetry That Forms Us

I am not a monk, and I imagine most of the people who read this book are neither monks nor nuns. That means, for most of us, that our lives do not include a regular, daily gathering of people who pray together, following a liturgy or ritual that gives voice to our common longing for God's blessing and presence.

But if we can accept the insight from Holy Cross Monastery—that a rhythm of regular prayers, even when rote or recited, is "like staring into eternity" and, furthermore, that our hearts are custodians of eternity given to us by God—then perhaps we might benefit from finding some way to introduce a rhythm of daily prayer into our lives.

According to the Italian philosopher Franco Berardi, "Language organizes time, space, and matter in such a way that they become recognizable to human consciousness." The language of prayer, therefore, opens our hearts to time, space, and reality in such a way that we more readily receive God's blessing and presence even though we may not consciously feel or experience the divine encounter as such. And while there is certainly value in using our own words when we pray, when we embrace the prayers we have received from our spiritual ancestors, we not only bond with them; we also are opened up to the divine encounter in a manner deeper than what we might be capable of managing or creating on our own. There is strength in numbers, including the "numbers" that stretch across the generations.

Many churches or religious orders have liturgical prayer books that anyone can use to begin a practice of daily prayer. Phyllis Tickle compiled a beautiful three-volume set of daily prayers called *The Divine Hours*; Shane Claiborne, Jonathan Wilson-Hartgrove, and Enuma Okoro collaborated on a one-volume breviary called *Common Prayer: A Liturgy for Ordinary Radicals*. The Northumbria Community, the Order of Saint Helena, and the Carmelites of Indianapolis have all published wonderful resources for daily prayer. If you are comfortable praying with your smartphone, apps such as iBreviary, Universalis, DivineOffice, or the Daily Office from Mission St. Clare give you the convenience of daily prayers right from your portable device.

You may enjoy visiting monasteries or convents where you can sit in the chapel and allow the chanting of the nuns or monks to wash over you as you rest in a kind of prayerful silence. Making the choice to pray daily fixed prayers on your own, especially in solitude, takes a greater commitment. It takes intentionality to remain mindfully present to the written prayers, neither rushing through them as if they didn't matter nor scrupulously trying to squeeze every ounce of meaning out of them. Liturgical prayer is like working out—it's not about making every single rep of whatever exercise you're doing matter so much as it is a choice to persevere with the exercise day in and day out, to allow your muscles to slowly grow, or in the case of the liturgy, to allow the words of praise and adoration for God to slowly shape and form your spirit in response to the silence of divine love.

Liturgical prayer, with its emphasis on chanting or reciting Psalms or other scriptural passages, may seem at odds with other elements of spiritual practice, such as silence or the imagination. Try to see silence and vocal prayer not as contradictory but as complementary, each illuminating spiritual truth in differing ways. Spoken prayer and silence belong together like a heartbeat and rest. Try to balance words and silence and trust the inner conversation among silence, image, and word.

Traditional prayers have been spoken or sung by the great mystics and contemplatives throughout history—especially the Psalms, which Jesus himself recited. Seek to pray such venerable words at least once a day or, if your schedule permits, more often than that. Remember, devout Muslims pray five times a day. More prayers won't make you holier, but just as a vigorous workout benefits us more than a half-hearted attempt, making the decision to show up with attentiveness and devotion when offering traditional prayers is a way of saying yes to God.

Does liturgical prayer get boring? Of course. Don't we all get bored with the quotidian tasks of our lives? But when we recall that our common prayers give us "space and no hurry at all" to gaze into the silence of eternity, hovering in and between the words we offer to God, even the most mundane words we pray may shimmer with the light of grace.

8

JOY

Few people have ever had such a transformative and dramatic conversion experience as the apostle Paul in the Bible. The story begins when he was still known as Saul, and he truly had a stony heart—he was someone dedicated to persecuting the Christians of the early church. A religious zealot, he devoted his energy to hunting down Christians, whom he regarded as dangerous schismatics, and turning them in to the authorities for their "crimes." Given a mandate to expand his reach, he went from Jerusalem to Damascus (over 125 miles away) to round up Christians and bring them before the religious establishment, where they would stand accused of heresy.

But while traveling the road to Damascus, Jesus appeared supernaturally to Saul, confronting him for his role in persecuting the Christians. This mystical encounter left Saul blinded but with instructions to undertake a healing journey to the Christians in Damascus. After convincing the Damascus believers of his changed heart and telling them of the vision on the road and the instruction to find the man who would help him regain his sight, Saul was transformed and his eyes healed. Eventually, Paul, as he came to be known, devoted his life to proclaiming the message of Jesus—a message of mercy and forgiveness and divine love—throughout the Roman Empire. That new zeal led to his own persecution, and eventually, tradition suggests, he was killed for his beliefs—but not before writing the letters that formed the heart of the New Testament.

For many people, the decision to embrace a conscious, chosen spiritual life is not nearly so dramatic—or traumatic. Perhaps for most of us, a spiritual awakening comes slowly over time. A spiritual conversion, or awakening, or enlightenment is rarely as startling and sensational as what happened to Paul. On the contrary, it seems most of us have multiple conversions—small and ordinary and undramatic moments in which, step by step, falling down and getting up again, we choose to align ourselves more and more with the heart of God.

Whether big or small, ordinary or life-defining, various moments of spiritual transformation keep coming in our lives even after we have made the big commitment to walk an intentional spiritual path—in whatever form it might take. That's certainly been my experience.

In fact, one of my most memorable "conversions" happened long after I made the decision to follow the path of Christ. This transforming moment took place sometime around my fiftieth birthday. By this point in my life, I had been a student of mysticism and contemplation for quite some time (I was writing *The Big Book of Christian Mysticism* about this time). But as this insightful incident illustrates, contemplative spirituality never stops offering us opportunities to grow.

This eye-opening moment came when I read a passage from the book *Prayer and Prophecy*, an anthology of writings from Kenneth Leech. "Contemplation has a context: it does not occur in a vacuum," he wrote. Leech continues, "Today's context is that of the multinational corporations, the arms race, the strong state, the economic crisis, urban decay, the growing racism, and human loneliness. It is within this highly deranged culture that contemplatives explore the waste of their own being. It is in the midst of chaos and crisis that they pursue the vision of God and experience the conflict which is at the core of the contemplative search."

The transforming, heart-expanding insight of these words helped me see prayer and contemplation from a new perspective. Having been a practitioner of silent forms of contemplative prayer for some time, I certainly was familiar with my prayer feeling chaotic—usually because my thought-frenzied mind just wouldn't slow down. Leech's insight opened my eyes to a deeper understanding. The reason prayer and other spiritual practices often feel chaotic, and attempts to be silent before God often result in discovering how noisy and distracted we are on the inside, stems from a truth so obvious that I had simply overlooked it: we live in a chaotic, noisy world. God doesn't call us into deep mystical spirituality just so we can have a blissful experience of God or take refuge in comfortable feelings of peace and serenity. If such feelings do arise, they are given to us only to empower, equip, and strengthen us for the good spiritual work we are called to do.

However we choose to pray—whether through words, or images, or simply silent love—we pray so that our lives may more fully manifest the radical, subversive, loving, merciful, forgiving, peacemaking, justice-building, reconciling, creative, caring, and fruitful vocation (calling) that God has placed in our hearts.

Everyone is called in a unique way to respond to the noise and the chaos of the world we inhabit. Too many people interested in contemplation and meditation get discouraged when they discover the "waste" within—the noise and tumult and disruption in their hearts and minds. But don't be dismayed by your inner turmoil, suggests Leech. Rather, take heart. You are called to enter into the most chaotic places in your heart, for that is precisely where you will discover the presence of God—the God who loves you and has been waiting for you since before the beginning of time.

The deeper we go, the more chaotic it gets because we live in an agitated world. And how can the hidden places within us be anything but chaotic? When we discover that our inner wasteland simply echoes and mirrors the outer wastelands in which our "contemplation has a context," we are liberated from the terrible temptation to judge our own prayer. At the same time, we find within ourselves the empowerment to bring healing and transformation both to our inner wasteland and also to the world we live in, a world so desperately hungry for the healing love of God.

What, then, is the final gift of the heart given to us as we persevere on this path into the treasures that God has poured into us?

It's not so much the last gift given, but it may be for many of us the ultimate gift we receive.

We acknowledged this gift at the very beginning of our journey, before we even embarked on the path. The final gift is the presence of the very Spirit of God.

Remember the words of the apostle Paul from his letter to the Romans: "Hope does not disappoint us, because God's love has been poured into our hearts through the Holy Spirit that has been given to us" (Romans 5:5). This is such a bold statement of how divine love is given to us (poured into our hearts, no less) that it would be easy to miss that this is simultaneously a proclamation that the Holy Spirit also is a gift placed graciously in our hearts.

I promised you eight gifts in our hearts. But it might be just as accurate to say that we receive seven gifts along with the giver of all the gifts. The seven gifts—the path, silence, law, new life, wisdom, love, and eternity—are preceded and followed by the greatest gift we might ever receive: God's own Spirit dwelling lavishly and generously in our hearts.

Julian of Norwich prayed, "God, of your goodness, give me yourself, for you are enough for me. I may ask nothing less that is fully to your worship, and if I do ask anything less, ever shall I be in want. Only in you I have all." God is the ultimate gift, for God is the ultimate source of life and love and grace. There is no greater request we can make of God than this: "give us the gift of yourself." And yet, as we make our journey through the heart—through all the gifts of the heart—what ultimately we discover is that each of these gifts is merely a facet of the One Gift, and each one is evidence that the One Gift has already been given to us since before there was a before.

If you have ever longed to feel God, to know God, to have a sense of divine presence or an awareness of union with God, the tremendous proclamation of the great mystics rings with one voice: the gift has already been given. You already have the fullness of the divine plenitude. You are already one with God. You do not have to earn it, or prove yourself worthy, or make gargantuan sacrifices, or perform acts of masochistic mortification. The very Spirit of God is already present in your heart—right here and right now.

Whether you feel that presence makes no difference. Whether you believe in it or not is immaterial. Whether you are a saint like Mother Teresa or your life is broken by sin and selfishness, either way you simply lack the power to banish God from your heart or change God's mind about you. For God loves you infinitely and unconditionally, and God has given and will continue to give divine love to you, delivered straight to your heart—abundantly, unconditionally, right here and right now.

> The seven gifts—the path, silence, law, new life, wisdom, love, and eternity—are preceded and followed by the greatest gift we might ever receive: God's own Spirit dwelling lavishly and generously in our hearts.

It's important to recognize that God has placed all the other gifts in our hearts. Learning to sense their presence prepares us to discover and acknowledge the greatest and ultimate gift. And while all the gifts of the heart point to God, I think the gifts of silence and eternity are especially important. Silence and eternity have this in common: they are both infinite in scope, which means they are big enough to hold God along with all the other heavenly gifts so graciously bestowed upon us.

"One should not think it impossible that the soul be capable of so sublime an activity as this breathing in God through participation as God breathes in her," notes John of the Cross, the great Spanish poet and mystic. He goes on to say, "God favors her by union with the Most Blessed Trinity, in which she becomes deiform and God through participation . . . thus the soul is like God through this transformation. He created her in his image and likeness that she might attain such resemblance." This is exalted teaching, so let's linger over what this great mystic is saying. God gives us the Holy Spirit, present in our hearts, so that we might restore our fullest and truest nature: our souls deified, from the Greek word θέωσις, *theosis*—literally, "transformed into God."

Whether we think so or not, and whether we feel anything "unitive" or not, God dwells in our hearts.

Perhaps to truly and fully realize this greatest gift, we need to once again rely on the imagination of the heart. If we can trust the good counsel of the apostle Paul and John of the Cross and so many other of the mystics and accept, even if just on faith, that the divine spirit is already present within us, then we can trust that the God who is present in our hearts can and will touch us through our imagination. Trusting that divine presence in our hearts and minds and spirits, we can imaginally visualize the splendor of mystical union with God.

At least one mediæval mystic had a beautiful, profound vision that illustrated her heart as the foundation of her divine union. Lutgarde of Aywières, a Cistercian nun, lived from 1182 to 1246. From childhood she was a mystic, and her earliest vision of Christ centered on what we would now call her Sacred Heart.

As Thomas Merton (who also was a Cistercian) recounts in his biography of Lutgarde, *What Are These Wounds?*, one day during her prayer, Christ appeared and asked her what she truly desired. She answered, in Latin, "Volo cor tuum" (I want your heart). But Jesus surprised her with his reply: "Actually, *I* want *your* heart." In this moment of mutual longing and desire, Lutgarde makes a profound offer: "So be it, Lord. But take my heart as your heart so that your love remains in my heart, for I give my heart only to you, trusting it to be kept safe forever under your protection."

Lutgarde's Latin is hard to unravel. She seems to be saying to Christ, "Yes, you may have my heart, for it belongs to you; to the extent that your love is poured into it, my heart *is* your heart—they are united as one."

Lutgarde challenges us to consider that the spiritual heart of Christ beats as one with our creaturely hearts—if not in a physical way, then certainly in a spiritual way. Perhaps we can meet Lutgarde's challenge with a prayer like this:

> Heavenly God, to fully know, and receive, and appreciate your divine presence in our lives, guide us to love as You love, show us how to see as You see, teach us to forgive as You forgive, inspire us to be creative as You are creative, direct us to manifest delight and felicity and beatitude and joy as You manifest all these, and most of all, through Your Spirit, may our hearts beat as Your heart—our two hearts beating as one. Amen.

This may sound like a daring, bold prayer. But the requests in this prayer follow the supplication of Lutgarde, who was responding to the spiritual truth that Christ desires union with us even more fully than we desire divine union with God.

This ultimate gift—the gift of divine presence—as most of us would wish it, would be nothing but delight and felicity. But even as the presence of God is ultimately the fountain of joy in our lives, the spiritual tradition teaches quite clearly that it carries its own cost. Paul was struck blind, remember? And never forget that Christ was crucified. What we see is that much of the language that surrounds the mystery of divine presence and union is rather frightening—language of death or annihilation, not to mention that cloud of unknowing.

Jesus taught clearly how nothing that lives eternally does so without first dying. He used a seed to illustrate this: being buried in the earth must come first, then the plant can burst forth with life.

Perhaps all that "dies" is the grasping ego, the self-conscious mental construction that insists the "I" remain always in control. When the "I" dies, that which it obscures—the grace-filled heart, the spirit, the soul, even the body—lives on, united with God. In other words, we live eternally united with Love.

This is the union with God that the mystics have proclaimed and celebrated, and this is the God each one of us is invited to welcome into our hearts—not just to "move in" like a tenant temporarily inhabits a leased house but to emerge resurrected in our hearts as we are resurrected into the divine nature, finding that the human heart and the divine heart are so deeply united that they are the same heart and have been all along, beating with one rhythm of love and silence, of joy and rest, of felicity and longing.

"All deities reside in the human breast," noted William Blake. Not just one deity (as in the One God) but "all" deities, which implies a type of spiritual diversity. His perspective invites us to consider an important question that some people might find threatening and others might find exciting in its possibilities. How are we to "meet" the wisdom of different faith traditions, even for those of us who are committed to one specific tradition? If I accept the Christian principle that the Holy Spirit resides in my heart, does that mean there is no room for other ways of experiencing or understanding the divine presence? Or, may I assume that all positive images of God point to One truth? Can I combine the depth of my commitment to following Christ with a broad, inclusive embrace of spiritual wisdom wherever it may arise?

I believe the answer to those last two questions is yes. Faithfulness to Christ and openness to the wisdom of other traditions are two aspects of my spiritual journey that have enhanced and enriched each other. When we embrace the divine presence in our hearts, it not only impels us into a deeper spiritual appreciation of our "home" spiritual tradition (in my case, Christianity) but also can help us identify how truth and insight resonate across spiritual traditions.

To illustrate this, I'd like to reflect on one passage in the New Testament that celebrates union with God, which also echoes a classic Buddhist text, the *Heart Sūtra*. The passage is Philippians 2:1–11:

> If then there is any encouragement in Christ, any consolation from love, any sharing in the Spirit, any compassion and sympathy, make my joy complete: be of the same mind, having the same love, being in full accord and of one mind. Do nothing from selfish ambition or conceit, but in humility

regard others as better than yourselves. Let each
of you look not to your own interests, but to the
interests of others. Let the same mind be in you
that was in Christ Jesus,

who, though he was in the form of God,
did not regard equality with God
as something to be exploited,
but emptied himself,
taking the form of a slave,
being born in human likeness.
And being found in human form,
he humbled himself
and became obedient to the point of death—
even death on a cross.

Therefore God also highly exalted him
and gave him the name
that is above every name,
so that at the name of Jesus
every knee should bend,
in heaven and on earth and under the earth,
and every tongue should confess
that Jesus Christ is Lord,
to the glory of God the Father.

Let's linger over this line: "be of the same mind, having
the same love, being in full accord and of one mind."
This same mind expresses and holds a unity of love, of

heart, and of consciousness. The Greek word for "the same mind" implies the consciousness that emerges from the interior of the body—the consciousness and understanding of the heart.

Paul says that what will make his joy complete is sharing with us the same will, the same embodiment, and the same knowing that he has encountered in Christ—in short, to be one with Christ. Until I began working on this book, I never understood just how nuanced this call to divine union truly is.

Let your Love be my love.

Let your Soul be my soul.

Let your Consciousness be my consciousness.

What a prayer. Yet that is precisely how Paul asks us to pray—so that his joy may be complete.

To illustrate this divine union, Paul offers insight into Christ's earthly journey—a journey shaped by kenosis (self-emptying) and humility. It eschews ambition and vainglory—a journey marked by radical letting-go, radical listening, radical self-forgetfulness.

Jesus emptied himself. He humbled himself. We are called to do the same. And in doing so, we become what we already are: one with him. One mind. One heart. One love. One knowing. In the words of the mediæval mystic Meister Eckhart, "The eye with which I see God is the same eye with which God sees me. My eye and God's eye is one eye, and one sight, and one knowledge, and one love."

The very mind of Christ *in* us, Paul writes. His language is important here: "*Let* the same mind . . ." It's an attitude of allowing, of receiving. We do not choose the mind of Christ; we receive it. It is pure grace; it is given to us. Our posture of prayer must be one of gentle receptivity.

What is "the mind of Christ"? I believe it is the gift of μετάνοια, *metanoia*—the Greek word for a concept we reflected on earlier, "repentance" in English which in a more literal sense means "to adopt a new consciousness." It means to be called beyond the limitations of a strictly human mind, which is the consciousness that creates suffering and sin. Yes, the Spirit calls us out of sin. But that call is not a guilt-trip; it's an invitation. It's a call to *a* new mind—beyond (*meta-*) the normal limitations of human consciousness and rationality. This is why, when atheists and agnostics tell me they think Christianity is irrational, I like to say, "Actually, it is *trans*rational."

The mind of Christ—the *-noia* of *metanoia*—is shaped by love rather than fear, by mercy rather than condemnation, by compassion rather than indifference, by generosity rather than parsimony. It is humble, loves to wonder, and is calibrated toward hope and joy. It is a nondualistic mind that loves unconditionally and remembers not to judge. It's a mind that sees through the eyes of God, eyes that love everyone equally (Matthew 5:45). It's a mind untainted by prejudice or

176 | Eternal Heart

bigotry or us-versus-them thinking. It's a mind of radical equality and inclusivity.

Paul takes us deeper into the consciousness of Christ by describing Christ's mystical journey from form into emptiness: "though he was in the form of God," he "emptied himself"—divesting himself of his divinity and "falling" (to use Julian of Norwich's evocative image) into Mary's womb, taking on human form. So we have a transition from the form of God, to emptiness, to human form.

Here is where I am reminded of the *Heart Sūtra*, one of the great Mahayana Buddhist sacred texts. The relevant line from the Red Pine translation reads, "Form is emptiness, emptiness is form; emptiness is not separate from form, form is not separate from emptiness; whatever is form is emptiness, whatever is emptiness is form."

Emptiness and *form* point to the basic impermanence of all things. Everything we see, we touch, we experience, even everything we know—it's all impermanent, it will all change. And because of this, the heart of all things (all "form") is emptiness.

You might be thinking, *Isn't God permanent?* Sure, but God is not the same thing as our image of God, our thoughts about God, our concept of God. All of those are impermanent. So even the form of God—as we know it—is essentially empty.

This is not a negation of truth; rather, it is a recognition that the kenosis (self-emptying) of Philippians 2 was not a one-off event. It is the way things eternally are. It is the nature of Christ to be emptied of the form of God. Form is emptiness. Out of that emptiness, Christ takes human form. Emptiness is form. And in doing so, Christ becomes obedient to death. Form is emptiness. Yet through death, Christ is exalted above all things. Emptiness is form.

We mere mortals are created in the image and likeness of God, so to the extent that we embrace the presence of Christ in us, we remain nonattached to our very selves. In doing this, our lives are not about having or accumulating but about loving and relating. We become nonattached to all things, and that nonattachment enables us to relate to others through love rather than through competition or grasping or hostility or defensiveness.

Because I am empty, I have nothing to defend.

Because I am undefended, I am available to receive, give, and literally *be* love.

Because my life is a participation in love, I am one with God.

Why am I devoting so much time and space to this interfaith exploration of spirituality? Couldn't I have made my point without trying to draw parallels between Buddhism and Christianity? Well, sure. But the age we live in is a time when the wisdom traditions of the world need to be in dialogue—which brings us to the beatitude I associate with this gift of divine presence: "Blessed are the peacemakers, for they will be called children of God" (Matthew 5:9).

It's one thing for peace to manifest in our lives as a fruit of the divine presence within us; it's another thing to actually become an agent of peace, a conduit through which the peace of God may flow to others.

Exploring the resonance between Philippians 2 and the *Heart Sūtra* illustrates just one type of peacemaking: fostering understanding and dialogue between religious traditions. That's important, yet it's hardly the only way we can make peace. For many of us, this is a calling to build communities of reconciliation—in our families, our neighborhoods, our churches, our communities, our nations, and the world at large. Peace can't sustainably exist without justice, so to be a peacemaker means also to be one committed to the struggle against injustice, oppression, systemic privilege, and harmful conflict wherever it emerges.

Once we truly recognize that the divine presence is in our hearts, that presence will impel us to grace others with love in many diverse ways: by practicing mercy and reconciliation, by fostering communities of justice and liberation, and by modeling all the fruits of the Spirit and the joy of all the beatitudes. And yes, by living life with passion, joy, and creativity.

The gifts of the heart bring us to a place of deep inner freedom and yet, paradoxically, a profound sense of responsibility toward God and toward all of God's creation. We become peacemakers out of a delightful desire to respond to the love within us—motivated by not duty or obligation but simply our innate desire to be living icons of love.

The gifts in our hearts invite us to a place of spiritual mastery where we may paradoxically become truly a servant of all. By seeing our inner wasteland in the light of divine love, we are empowered to gaze honestly and undefensively at the external wasteland in which we live, and we find ourselves overwhelmed by the call to make things better. How? Perhaps it is as simple as kneeling to wash one another's feet.

In reaching the end of the heart's path, we realize it is but the beginning. We are filled with the fullness of God only so that we may give it away. We look for ways to serve, to care, to make peace, to foster justice. We struggle against the forces of evil and fear by investing our lives and our energies in the service of goodness, hope, and love. And in doing all of this, without even realizing it, we find that perhaps the most wondrous fruit of the Spirit bountifully emerges in our hearts.

Joy.

> **We become nonattached to all things, and that nonattachment enables us to relate to others through love rather than through competition or grasping or hostility or defensiveness.**

When we embrace our union with the divine presence, we do not just make the apostle Paul's joy complete. We also fully manifest our own joy.

Joy is not the same thing as amusement or fun or entertainment. Not that there is necessarily anything wrong with those things, but they tend to be transitory—often merely endeavors that ultimately leave the heart restless. Joy is the felicity and delight that comes purely from God. The Greek word for joy, χαρά, chara, is related to the word for grace, χάρις, charis. Grace is the gift of unmerited favor and delight from God; joy, therefore, is the means by which we receive that gift and allow it to form our lives. Beyond just a light and exuberant feeling, joy is a foundational orientation of our hearts and minds—toward God, toward love, toward grace, toward hope, toward life. The happy feelings that we commonly think of as joyful are ordinary side effects of this deep interior transformation, but the transformation can be given, and remain an essential part of us, even when our mercurial feelings come and go. We know that human emotions are fickle and often reactive to external circumstances, just like our monkey-mind thoughts. When we receive the gifts in our hearts—and give our hearts back to the divine presence within—then joy becomes the foundation of all our feelings just as surely as silence is the foundation of the stream of thinking consciousness.

Many people suffer profound obstacles to truly knowing and experiencing such divine joy. Sometimes we have been so deeply hurt by life or are so infected with cynicism and rage and bitterness that to truly receive joy and give ourselves fully to it seems almost impossible. When it seems like joy is impossible, we are tempted to despair. But just as the only thing stronger than death is love, so too the force that will ultimately overcome hopelessness is joy. In the wisdom of Parker J. Palmer, "The joy beyond despair comes when we abandon the exhausting illusion of self-sufficiency and become the grateful recipients of the gifts that life provides." Joy naturally emerges when despair is healed, and the "medicine" for such healing is the grace of God.

Imagine that grace—the divine medicine—functions as an intravenous drip. And indeed, if the medicine were given to us all at once, it might be more than we can bear. The Holy Spirit, in her gracious wisdom, gives us a leisurely drip of grace, slowly and almost imperceptibly, so that little by little, we might root out the infection of fear and rage and woundedness and sin. We have to be gentle with the process, for sometimes it takes time—a lot of time.

It's all in your heart. Everything you need to find your way directly into that divine presence is there as well. You are merely finding your way into a blessing that is already given.

But when we say yes to the gifts of the Holy Spirit, we have embraced the process. Once the healing begins, moments of delight and beatitude will arrive unexpectedly. Glimmers of the luminous wonder that awaits us, as our hearts become more fully immersed in the heart of God, will be revealed to us, glimpse by hopeful glimpse. We can trust love. We can trust mercy. We can trust the spirit of life, a spirit that will heal us and make us whole and then inspire us to bring love and care to others so that one by one, we can slowly transform the entire world.

We began our journey with the wisdom of Saint Benedict: "the divine presence is everywhere." Even in our hearts. Let's finish our journey (which is really just beginning the next adventure) with one final word from dear Julian of Norwich, who linked the all-pervasive divine presence with her understanding of prayer and with the fruit of *chara*: "For the fullness of joy is to behold God in all."

It's all in your heart. Everything you need to find your way directly into that divine presence is there as well. You are merely finding your way into a blessing that is already given. Accept the gift, exult in it, and then share it with the world. The more you give it away, the more it flows within you. Joy, like love, multiplies as we share it with others. May we all orient our lives to such an economy of grace.

Heart Practice:
Embracing the Way of Silent Love

We began our journey along the path of the heart by acknowledging that there is really only one spiritual practice: prayer. So for this final practice, let's revisit prayer as the core spiritual exercise for our ongoing journey into joy.

Many different spiritual teachers and traditions of contemplative wisdom have emphasized silence and the imagination as foundations for prayer. Ignatius of Loyola, founder of the Jesuits and the creator of the *Spiritual Exercises*, made an imaginal encounter with Christ in prayer a central practice of his spiritual exercises. The anonymous author of *The Cloud of Unknowing* taught a practice grounded in deep silence and an imageless way of praying.

Like so many other elements of the spiritual life, in this tension, we find a paradox, with two complementary approaches to spirituality: the *kataphatic* (wordfull) approach and the *apophatic* (wordless) approach. Kataphatic spirituality finds a path to God through language and images; it celebrates the imagination as a powerful interior tool for meeting God within. Apophatic spirituality, by contrast, meets God by setting all language and images aside, choosing darkness over light, silence over language, and emptiness over imagery.

As complementary practices, neither silence nor the imagination is necessarily better or higher than the other.

A more pertinent question is, Which approach to God is right *for you*—and right for you today, at this time? (Five or twenty-five years from now, you may want or need a different approach.)

In chapter 2, we explored meditation as a practice for entering imaginal space, but now I invite you to balance your imaginative prayer with a willingness to step into silence and interior imagelessness: to meditate in the cloud of unknowing. Here, instead of cultivating a vivid imagination, take the time to allow your imagination to rest, and simply rest in the silence, where you encounter nothing but the love of God.

For some people, praying with the imagination is incredibly challenging, but resting in silence seems effortlessly simple. If you are like this, then hopefully you can embrace this idea of silence as prayer and make it a regular part of your spiritual discipline. On the other hand, you might find that imaginal prayer is richly rewarding for you, whereas attempting to meet God in silence feels like an endless frustration. While I hope you will at least try to embrace the divine presence in silence, I encourage you to remain with the kind of prayer that most easily fits your personality. And if you are one of the lucky ones who finds both imaginal prayer and silent prayer nourishing, then give yourself a balanced diet: find time for both silence and imaginative prayer on a regular, ideally daily, basis.

Why does prayer matter? If God is already in our hearts, why pray? For the same reason that a mother pays attention to the baby in her womb. Being intimately present does not render communication unnecessary. Human beings are creatures who relate, and we relate through doing and being, through action and contemplation, through speaking and listening. And when it comes to God, we communicate through imagining and resting in silence. Some of us prefer one way or another, and that's fine. But we all need to pray in some way—doing so will simply strengthen the bond and help us be more conscious and cognizant of the gift of divine presence so generously poured into us.

Take time to be silent in the presence of God—today and every day. Let me close with a quote from a renowned Orthodox contemplative, Theophan the Recluse: "What then is prayer? Prayer is the raising of the mind and heart to God in praise and thanksgiving. . . . The essence of prayer is therefore the spiritual lifting of the heart towards God. The mind in the heart stands consciously before the face of God, filled with due reverence, and begins to pour itself out before Him. This is spiritual prayer, and all prayer should be of this nature."

∞

COURAGE

One night I dreamt that I was driving home.

I was driving in the eastern suburbs of Atlanta, heading toward my home near the town of Clarkston. From Church Street, I turned left onto Northern Avenue, where I would drive about three-fourths of a mile before coming to the verdant, forested neighborhood where Fran and I live.

As I drove down Northern Avenue, something shifted in my dreamspace, and it was no longer "my" road but rather an unfamiliar street in an imaginal space. This often happens to me in dreams, and I suspect it often happens to you as well. As can happen in the dream-world, at first, I didn't realize this shift had occurred.

I drove a way through a beautiful residential neighborhood with plenty of well-tended green lawns and leafy mature trees. The road took me over rolling hilltops and curved gently here and there. Without consciously realizing it, I began to drive faster and faster. Then I looked at my speedometer. I was going sixty-nine—almost double the street's thirty-five-miles-per-hour speed limit.

I know I often zip along as I travel through this suburban forest, but this felt way too fast, even for me. I wanted to slow down, but I didn't just pump the breaks. Part of me wanted to keep going as fast as I could, while another, perhaps more sensible part knew I needed to decelerate. I gently raised my foot off the gas pedal in order to slow down—just a little bit at first. The speedometer reading changed from sixty-nine, to sixty-seven, to about sixty-five or so; I could see I wasn't slowing down fast enough (as I write these words, I'm amused at the inner paradox). I eased up my foot altogether from the accelerator and allowed the car to coast, gradually slowing down, as I continued to drive along the hills and curves of what I still imagined was the road home.

Then I rounded a sharper curve right by the empty lot that, over a decade ago, had been purchased to set up a school for refugee children, but along this dreamworld Northern Avenue, that lot was no longer there. In its place, I suddenly saw a large body of water—like the ocean, perhaps, or a great lake, or maybe even a Scottish loch. Surf sprayed along a rocky shoreline just a few feet away and below the edge of the pavement. As beautiful as the water was, it's not what grabbed my attention. What I did see, all around me, were children—probably anywhere from eight to fourteen years old—two dozen or more of them, all floating and flying around and above me in a colorful assortment of paragliders.

I slowed the car down so I could marvel at what I saw. The water, to my left, kept crashing against the rocks beneath the road, and I could see that the kids were launching their paragliders right there on the shoreline, where the offshore breeze was strong enough to suddenly push them up into the sky. Not too high, maybe just thirty or forty feet or so, but enough that they could, for just a few giddy moments, *fly*. And indeed, they flew! Above me, around me, to both my right and my left, circling and dancing in the sky, diving and spinning, above the water, above the road, and landing in a field to my right. And then, as soon as they landed, they would pick up their paragliders and run across the road to the shore to catch the wind and ascend again.

In this imaginal dreamspace, some of the kids even flew paragliders that could accommodate two passengers—"doubles" or "two-seaters," if you will, with long bars that the children could sit on as they rode their magic sailing ships up above the road. I was close enough to see their smiles and faces glowing with delight. While some flew tandem with friends or classmates, others rode solo, navigating their little aircraft all by themselves. The wings of the paragliders featured every color you could imagine, a rainbow of delight filling the sky.

I drove through this prismatic array of girls and boys flying joyously, and if the water wasn't clue enough that I had entered a nonordinary neighborhood, the road came to an abrupt end, where the tarmac gave way to a field of grass. I had reached the end of the mainland, water now on both sides, and only a small grassy isthmus stretched out ahead of me. It was so narrow that it seemed better for walking than for driving; I could have driven on it if I had wanted, but once I left the mainland, it would have been too narrow to turn my car around. I wanted to go home, so I turned my vehicle around, there at the very end of the road, and then slowly—yes, slowly—made my way back, under and among the colorful kids who continued to fly.

As I drove beneath them, I thought, *Wouldn't it have been nice if this opportunity had existed when I was a boy?* But then another, more melancholy thought occurred to me: *If it had, I would have been too scared to do it.* Flashes of childhood anxiety danced through my mind, like when, in the first grade, I was too timid to play on a spiral slide because it looked too tall or when my friend Chris would walk over an exposed pipe that crossed a ravine, but I held back, afraid I would lose my balance and fall. I felt like I was one of the people starving at Auntie Mame's banquet. I took a deep breath and put those thoughts out of my mind, but not after feeling a pang of sadness. Then I drove off . . . and woke up to a new dawn.

Do dreams come from the mind or from the heart?

I have always thought that it is the mind that dreams; the brain that constructs the spaces we inhabit when we sleep. But lately, I'm not so sure that dreams arise merely from the mind.

Our journey along the path of the heart has invited us to befriend the visionary, imaginal spaces within. And what can be more imaginal than a dream? As my dreams arise, it seems that they come from somewhere deeper—or higher.

This notion of imaginal consciousness shows up again and again in the world's mystical traditions. I encounter it in shamanic wisdom, in Sufi mysticism, or in the esoteric adventures of people like G. I. Gurdjieff or Cynthia Bourgeault. Like so many aspects of mystical spirituality, this visionary realm seems impossible to put into words. Whatever I say about it will simultaneously be as true as the love of God and as distorted as any human blind spot can be. When it comes to dreamspace, we are all blind persons groping at the elephant, a reminder for us all to remain humble.

The dreamspace in our hearts is an arena where the frontiers of human thought and imagination pour bracingly into the vast mystery of divine love and creativity. Every one of us explores this space every night when we sleep. Sometimes—often—we stay close to shore, and the imaginings of our dreams are hardly more than reruns of the images and thoughts and feelings that flittered through our conscious the day (or decade) before.

Each of us, in our own imaginal space, has a kind of subjective "home page" where we can take refuge in what is known, what is familiar, what is remembered and loved (or feared and repressed, for those things too have a way of showing up in both dreams and deep meditation). But just as Northern Avenue suddenly phased into a road I had never driven down before, taking me to a place filled with wonder and delight, so it is that every human imaginal consciousness is but a tributary to the great ocean of divine creativity.

There are cul-de-sacs and detours along the way, of course, which is another reason why I have come to believe that dreams belong to the heart rather than the mind. An authority no less than Cinderella once proclaimed, "A dream is a wish your heart makes." Sometimes, and sometimes in a flash, our dreams become nightmares, and the happiness turns into unspeakable terror. After my daughter died, nightmares terrorized me night after night. It's as if every evening, my heart gave me permission to face just a little bit more of my own deep grief and angst as I gazed into the abyss of loss—and my own mortality. Had I tried to process all this at once, I probably would have ceased to function in response to life's daily needs. A dream may be our hearts' wish, but a nightmare is our hearts' processing of whatever shadow material simply needs to be faced at that particular subconscious moment.

Someone once told me that the feeling, the emotional resonance, within a dream matters more than what images or symbols might pop up in it. Different schools of thought (and paperback dream dictionaries) try to tell us what our dreams "mean" in a kind of dogmatic attempt to manage the imaginal miracle that emerges when we sleep. Flying symbolizes freedom, water symbolizes the unconscious—that sort of thing.

The mind may accept such symbolic definitions from this or that dream authority. But thankfully, the heart does not submit so easily. The dream that looks like paradise but feels like hell (or vice versa) has something very important to tell us. And the message is coming from the heart.

Like my dream so blatantly pointed out, I have a lifelong fear of falling, impacting me in big ways and small. Spiritually speaking, the fear seems to point to a profound anxiety about being separated from God. Of course, "I fall down, and I get back up." The fear is never the last word. But it still is a challenge that must be faced on the journey to wisdom.

As someone who has struggled with, and learned to overcome, fears that can hold us back from even life's simple pleasures, I have considered three ways we can respond. The first way involves *hope*. Every time we feel fear, we have the option of reframing it as hope. "I fear I am going to lose my job" can be reframed as "I hope I am successful in my career." "I fear that my wife will leave me" can be reframed as "I hope I am a good and loving husband." These examples show the nature of hope—and how it tends to be more proactive than fear. Fear often has to do with something happening to me: "I'm afraid I'll be laughed at" or "I'm afraid I'll be abandoned." Hope, by contrast, involves making wise choices and commitments so as to create the best possible life for myself: "I hope I'll take good care of myself" or "I hope I'll be compassionate and loving in my relationships." Hope by itself cannot prevent misfortune from occurring; I might still get laid off or my marriage might break down. But if I am facing life's uncertainty with hope rather than fear, I am empowered to make choices that can help me move on even when misfortune strikes.

Hope by itself is merely a wish, but it creates more possibility for action than fear ever does. And when we act on the basis of our hopes, we access the potential of generating the life we truly want.

Hope comes from God; hope originates in God. We've seen how the apostle Paul, in his letter to the Romans, intimately associated hope with both the love and presence of God: "Hope does not disappoint us, because God's love has been poured into our hearts through the Holy Spirit that has been given to us" (Romans 5:5). That we are capable of hoping at all— even about the smallest of things—is evidence that the Holy Spirit of God is resident in our hearts and active in our lives.

You might respond, "But I'm not a very hopeful person." The fact that you exist, that you are here to read these words of hope—and even conceive of hope—points to the Holy Spirit present in you, loving you. "I think, therefore I am," mused the philosopher Descartes. The mystical corollary goes a little differently: "I exist, therefore God loves me." This logically leads to "God loves me, therefore I can hope."

When we tap into the hope in our hearts, fear begins to lose its hold on us. Our task when facing fear is to find the hidden hope and give it our attention and our energy: "I'm afraid of dying" becomes "I hope to live life for the fullest, even if only for today."

I have worked for many years on this practice of recalibrating my fears into hopes. I've come to recognize that I still often faced the future looking through the eyes of fear rather than the eyes of faith. When I became self-employed, this became painfully obvious. Every time I experienced a professional or financial setback—say, I lost a client or a speaking engagement was canceled—my fear kicked into hyperdrive, and I thought that was surely evidence of my imminent

failure. But when, two days later, an even better opportunity suddenly showed up, did I interpret it as "clear
evidence of my ongoing success"? I'm afraid not.

When I began to notice this pattern, I realized that
my existential fear was so deeply rooted in my mind
that even repeated applications of hope were not root-
ing it out. I needed something that worked in tandem
with hope—I needed *trust*.

Hope, as I've said, invites us to action; hope gave
me the energy to take positive steps or make positive
changes. Trust brings in relationality, which means that
it is embedded in nurturing a relationship with God
and others. To the person of faith, trust is anchored
in our relationship with God—with God's goodness,
God's mercy, and God's providence.

When I feared bad things might happen to me, I
began to see it as a signal that I needed to cultivate
a deeper trust in God. I needed to recognize that in
the grand scope of things, sometimes bad things really
do happen (I am writing these words in the midst of
the 2020 coronavirus pandemic, in which hundreds
of thousands of people are getting sick and dying from
a virus that no one had even heard of until recently). Yet
through hope strengthened by trust, we are equipped to
deal responsibly and prudently when bad things happen
while also being capable of fully cherishing and enjoy-
ing life's many blessings. Simply put, trust—the ability

to count on the goodness of God—makes everything better.

As much as hope and trust have helped me overcome the limitations of my fears, one more virtue or quality proved necessary to manage and assuage my fears: *courage*.

God bless Bert Lahr, the cowardly lion who sang in his exaggerated Brooklyn accent, "If I only had the noive!" We equate courage with "the nerve" because we intuitively know that courage is a profoundly embodied virtue: if hope is reframing the emotion of fear, and trust is anchoring our lives in relationship with God, then courage is placing our full personhood, body as well as soul, in the service of life at a place deeper than fear. Courage literally means "having heart"—a person of courage knows that our bodies, our nerves, and our hearts must all join together to say no to fear and yes to faith. We can't just think our way out of fear. And while trusting in God is essential, we have to put that trust into embodied action. We have to show up with our hearts and act on our hopes. That's what courage is.

Hope invites us to action, giving energy to make positive changes. Trust brings in relationality, which means it is embedded in nurturing a relationship with God and others.

In his wonderful *Meditations on the Heart*, Howard Thurman reflects on courage. "Courage is not a blustering manifestation of strength and power," he muses. "Sometimes courage is only revealed in the midst of great weakness and fear." But he goes on to connect the dots between courage and the heart: "There is a quiet courage that comes from an inward spring of confidence in the meaning and significance of life. Such courage is an underground river, flowing far beneath the shifting events of one's experience . . . it is best seen in the lives of men and women who do their work from day to day without hurry and without fever."

Like everything else we have reflected on during our hearts' journey, courage is a gift. We access this gift by finding those places in our hearts where we can let go of hurry and worry, settling into the stillness between each heartbeat and perhaps even touching the face of eternity in the silence. Moment by moment, our hearts keep beating; the silence keeps yielding to pumping blood and purposeful thought and all that impels us into "the meaning and significance of life." Courage is the expression of a heart that is calibrated to all the gifts and promises and fruits that we have explored. Our eternal, wise, loving, deiform, discerning, renewed, beating hearts—immersed in silence and mapped with a pathway to joy—are innately courageous. And the more we learn to live from the abundance of the gifts given, the more we will meet life's promises and problems from a place of courage rather than fear, hope rather than anxiety, trust rather than cynicism. Our eternal hearts contain all that we need for a joyful, loving, and truly meaningful life.

The courage to live a joyful life is a gift available to every one of us, no matter how much suffering or trauma life may deal us. As Jim Morrison pointed out, no one here gets out alive—no one escapes at least some measure of suffering, or hardship, or trauma. Likewise, joy and delight are gifts available to even the most stone-cold, fear-ridden heart. The reason for this is elegant in its simplicity: joy, being a fruit of the Spirit, comes to us from God, not from our own achievements or earnings or the random fortunes bestowed upon us by family or society.

Joy does not make sorrow or suffering or trauma disappear. It is not a panacea, a miracle drug that eliminates pain or grief or fear. It does not abdicate us of our responsibility to be kind, compassionate, merciful people who work for justice and equality. The more joy becomes rooted in our hearts, the more we will be inspired, called, perhaps even impelled to give our lives away in love and service to others.

What difference does a joyful, courageous, mystical life make? It creates space within us—space for the three antidotes to fear (hope, trust, and courage), space for faith, space for caring, space for compassion and mercy and forgiveness, space for prayer and delight. It inspires us to live under the guidance of love, for self as well as for others.

Benedict talks about how our hearts expand as we travel the pathway into the heart of God. Joy is the mystical agent by which our hearts expand. And as our hearts expand, grace and divine love and, indeed, the presence of the Holy Spirit simply fill us all the more. We are filled to overflowing so that we naturally and instinctually share that divine presence and love with others in ways both large and small.

The journey of the heart is an adventure of a lifetime and beyond. To infinity and beyond. Let's go—whenever you're ready.

ACKNOWLEDGMENTS

Portions of this book originally appeared (in slightly different form) in my blog, www.anamchara.com. My online course, Promises of the Heart, offered through Spirituality and Practice, was an opportunity for me to explore some of the ideas found here.

Many people have contributed in ways small and large to the process by which this book was dreamed, imagined, and written into being. Particular gratitude goes to Linda Boland; Lerita Coleman Brown, PhD; Patricia Campbell Carlson; Lil Copan; Brittany Cyr; Phil Foster; Cassidy Hall; Cindy Lou Harrington; Elias Marechal, OCSO; Marie Howe; Kevin Johnson; Linda Mitchell; Andy Otto; Fr. Aidan Owen, OHC; Sr. LaVerne Peter, WSHS; Linda Roghaar; and Laura Sorrells. For spiritual support, I am thankful for Fr. Mark Horak, SJ; Fr. Tim Stephens, SJ; Kay Satterfield; Maggie Winfrey; and everyone in the St. Thomas More Wednesday night Centering Prayer group and in the Lay Cistercians of Our Lady of the Holy Spirit. A particular bow of gratitude goes to all the patrons and benefactors who support my writing ministry through Patreon—you truly have made this book possible. Finally, as always, I can only express joy and wonder at the continual care and love I receive so lavishly from my wife and best friend, Fran McColman. Fran, you make my eternal heart sing.

Carl McColman
Feast of Blessed Jan van Ruusbroec, 2020

NOTES

Some of the quotations in this book have been adapted for the purpose of inclusive language.

0
Infinity

William Blake's poem "Auguries of Innocence" begins with the line "To see a world in a grain of sand." It was written around the year 1803 but not published until after the poet's death. To my mind, the worst song the Beatles ever recorded (if you can call it a song) is "Revolution 9," found on their self-titled album *The Beatles*, popularly known as the "White Album." Thich Nhat Hanh discusses the concept of interbeing in many of his books. If you're new to him, try *Living Buddha, Living Christ* for starters. The song "We Are All Made of Stars" was written by Moby to express hope after the horror of the 9/11 attacks. It appears on his album *18*. Shunryu Suzuki's concept of "beginner's mind" is immortalized in his book *Zen Mind, Beginner's Mind*. The TARDIS,

Doctor Who's "vehicle" for traveling through space and time, famously resembles a British police box and is renowned for being bigger on the inside than the outside. To hear Buzz Lightyear's catchphrase, watch the first *Toy Story* movie, released in 1995.

1
Passage

Quotes on the divine presence come from *The Rule of Saint Benedict* (chapter 19), *The Confessions of Saint Augustine* (book 3, chapter 6, p. 30), *The Showings of Julian of Norwich* (chapter 11 of the long text), *The Spiritual Exercises of Saint Ignatius* (#235), and the Letters of Ignatius, #240. *The Cloud of Unknowing*, by an anonymous author, probably a Carthusian monk, was written in Middle English around the year 1375. Thomas Keating, OCSO, wrote many books on the practice of Centering Prayer, a form of silent meditation based on *The Cloud of Unknowing* and other ancient texts. Krishnamurti's famous line "Truth is a pathless land" was proclaimed during his "Dissolution Speech" of August 3, 1929. It's ironic that the young philosopher rejected spiritual institutions as crippling to human freedom, and yet his work continues to be shepherded by a foundation that bears his name. John O'Donohue's idea of the spiritual journey being just a quarter-inch long is found in *Anam Ċara: A Book of Celtic Wisdom*. Henry David Thoreau's wisdom comes to us from *Walden*. Julian of Norwich's thoughts on prayer as "seeking" and "beholding" are found in chapter 10 of her long text.

2
Silence

Thomas Keating speaks of silence as God's first language in *Invitation to Love: The Way of Christian Contemplation*. In chapter 6 of *The Cloud of Unknowing*, the author makes the case for the heart being more capable than the mind for encountering God. Mirabai's poems, such as "Your Look of Light," can be found in *The Poetry of Mirabai: "Don't Forget Love; It Will Bring All the Madness You Need."* William Blake's thoughts on the imagination come from *The Marriage of Heaven and Hell*. Peter Gabriel's song "Mercy Street" appears on his album *So*.

3
Discernment

The Worker Sisters and Brothers of the Holy Spirit are online at www.workersisters.org. Some of the books I read while researching the Jewish background of Jesus (and Jewish spirituality today) include *Jesus: The Misunderstood Jew* and *Short Stories by Jesus* by Amy-Jill Levine, *The Sabbath* by Abraham Joshua Heschel, *Liberating the Gospels: Reading the Bible with Jewish Eyes* by John Shelby Spong, *Jewish Spirituality: A Brief Introduction for Christians* and *Honey from the Rock* by Lawrence Kushner, *Living Judaism* by Wayne D. Dosick, *What Every Christian Needs to Know about the Jewishness of Jesus* by Rabbi Evan Moffic, and *The Jewish Annotated New Testament* edited by Amy-Jill Levine and Marc Zvi Brettler. "If I can't dance, I don't want to be part of your revolution" is often attributed to Emma Goldman; she didn't say it in so many words but does express the basic sentiment in her autobiography, *Living My Life*. Cindy Lou Harrington's song "Language of the Heart" comes from her 1993 album, also called *Language of the Heart*. Thomas Merton's thoughts on imagination can be found in a recording of Merton lecturing on the poetry of Rilke, "'God Speaks to Each of Us': The Poetry and Letters of Rainer Maria Rilke," recorded on November 14, 1965. The recording is available through Now You Know Media. Martin Luther King Jr.'s "I Have a Dream" speech may be found online at https://tinyurl.com/l5ftd36 (accessed November 6, 2020).

4
Renewal

I share more about my relationship with Rhiannon, who passed away in 2014, in the first chapter of *Unteachable Lessons*. John Bradshaw offers insight into shame in his book *Healing the Shame That Binds You*. Bob Hamp provides a balanced reflection on Jeremiah 17:9 at https://tinyurl.com/yymmme5z (accessed November 6, 2020). If you are interested in the spirituality of undergoing a heart transplant, read *When the Heart Speaks, Listen* by Lerita Coleman Brown, PhD. It is a brilliant, warm, and at times quietly amusing book about what it means to surrender a dying heart—and welcome a new heart into one's life. The story of Howard Thurman's encounter with racists on the train is recounted in *Jesus and the Disinherited*. Sylvia Boorstein's thoughts on compassion are found in *It's Easier Than You Think: The Buddhist Way to Happiness*. André Louf's brilliant reflection on the spirituality of asceticism is found in *The Cistercian Way*.

5
Wisdom

As noted previously, I write more about Rhiannon's story in *Unteachable Lessons*. I also write in that book about the relationship between generosity and trust. Caryll Houselander's *The Reed of God*, Henri Nouwen's *The Wounded Healer*, and Rabbi Zalman Schachter-Shalomi's *Gate to the Heart* are examples of down-to-earth twentieth-century mystical writing. John Lennon's cynical song "God" is found on his first solo album, *Plastic Ono Band*. It's not a sunshiny album like most Beatles records—just saying. Benedict's words on welcoming guests as Christ can be found in chapter 53 of his *Rule*.

6

Love

Learn about Zentangle by visiting www.zentangle .com. The image of the child being asked to speak to Grandma on the telephone is based on a monologue in Laurie Anderson's brilliant two-night performance art concert *United States*, which I saw in 1984. John of the Cross's poem "Living Flame of Love" became the foundation of one of his most sublime works of mystical theology, also called *The Living Flame of Love*. Benedict's comment about the expanding heart appears in the prologue to the *Rule of Saint Benedict*. The wisdom of Rumi and Rabia can be found in *The Essential Rumi* and Daniel Ladinsky's wonderful anthology *Love Poems from God*. Julian of Norwich's comments about the soul in the heart come from her sixteenth showing (chapter 67 of her long text). John O'Donohue's comments about the soul and the body can be found on his audiobook, *Anam Ċara: Wisdom from the Celtic World*.

7
Eternity

I tell the story of how my Muslim friend inspired me to be a better practitioner of Christian prayer in *Unteachable Lessons*. Starhawk's comments on ritual come from her book *Dreaming the Dark*. "We never blow our trip forever" is an allusion to the Franco-British avant-garde band Gong, whose song "You Never Blow Yr Trip Forever" appeared on their 1974 album *You*. John Wesley wrote about his remarkable experience of his "heart strangely warmed" in his journal; you can read it in *John and Charles Wesley: Selected Prayers, Hymns, Journal Notes, Sermons, Letters and Treatises*. The insights of Thea Bowman have been collected in *Thea Bowman in My Own Words*. The wisdom of Makarios was compiled by Igumen Chariton of Valamo in his book *The Art of Prayer: An Orthodox Anthology*. Kenneth Leech's profound teaching on the subversive nature of contemplation is found in *The Social God* and reprinted in *Prayer and Prophecy: The Essential Kenneth Leech*. Franco "Bifo" Berardi's fascinating ideas about language can be found in *Breathing: Chaos and Poetry*.

8

Joy

As mentioned previously, Leech's words on contemplation were originally found in *The Social God* and are also included in *Prayer and Prophecy*. Julian of Norwich's prayer is found in chapter 5 of her long text. To learn more about Lutgarde of Aywières, read Thomas Merton's *What Are These Wounds?* and also Bernard McGinn's *The Great Cistercian Mystics: A History*. John of the Cross speaks about becoming "deiform" in his *Spiritual Canticle*, section 39.4, which is found in *The Collected Works of St. John of the Cross*. William Blake's comment about deities residing in the human breast comes from *The Marriage of Heaven and Hell*. The statement about "my faithfulness to Christ and my openness to the wisdom of other traditions" is a direct quote from my first book, *Spirituality: Where Body and Soul Encounter the Sacred*, published in 1997. Meister Eckhart's comment about the "one eye" can be found in his Sermon #16. The phrase "radical equality and inclusivity" comes from the Trappist monk Elias Marechal, author of *Tears of an Innocent God*. The Red Pine translation of the *Heart Sūtra* was published by

Counterpoint in 2004. Parker J. Palmer's insights into joy and despair come from his book *The Active Life*. Theophan the Recluse's wisdom is found in Igumen Chariton of Valamo's *The Art of Prayer: An Orthodox Anthology*.

∞

Courage

A wonderful book for exploring imaginal conscious-ness is Cynthia Bourgeault's *The Eye of the Heart*. Based on the teachings of G. I. Gurdjieff, it weaves together Christian and esoteric forms of mysticism to proclaim a beautiful, inclusive expression of spirituality. I also write about my ongoing journey from fear to trust in the final chapter of *Unteachable Lessons*. Jim Morrison sings "No one here gets out alive" in the Doors song "Five to One," from the album *Waiting for the Sun*.